Enclosure

A Spiritual Autobiography

Daina,

Angels are all around you!
Talk with us every morning
and we will work with
you and guide you for
the best & perfect outcome
in every situation &
relationship!
Love, Barbara Becker

BARBARA BECKER

ISBN: 1470048752
ISBN-13: 9781470048754

Library of Congress Control Number: 2012920553
CreateSpace Independent Publishing Platform
North Charleston, South Carolina

Photograph of Barbara Becker by Jesse Sparks

I dedicate this book to my Angels and Guides.

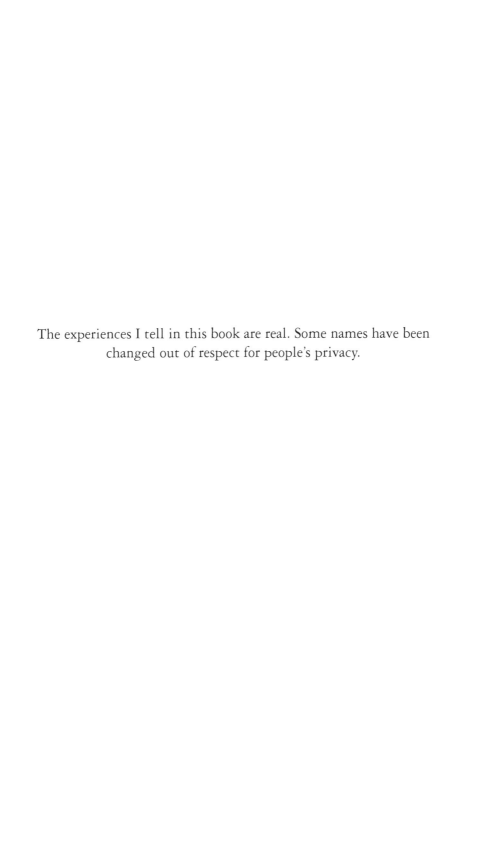

The experiences I tell in this book are real. Some names have been changed out of respect for people's privacy.

ACKNOWLEDGMENTS

I am grateful for the expertise and guidance from my CreateSpace project teams, my guides on the other side, my most Holy Guardian Angel, and the Ascended Masters' encouragement and support. My infinite love and gratitude to Grandmaster Zaysan, Dr. Peebles, Shaman Lance Heard, Elizabeth Kuester, Ann Albers, Summer Bacon, Jenny Cohen, Hoyt L.Kesterson, II, Jesse Sparks, Diana Hutchinson, Peter Nufer, my family, and my Tai Chi classmates.

TABLE OF CONTENTS

INTRODUCTION

by Elizabeth Kuester
channeled through Barbara Becker

Cool, cool, cool, Barb! I am here. I am here...

When we are children, we are open to the possibilities and fantasies of our imagination. We are able to see and communicate with spirits. Usually, by age seven, we "turn off" these innate abilities, due to repetitive negative reinforcement from our public education system, our parents, religious dogma, and the medical community. This negative reinforcement is accomplished with fear, punishment, judgment, medications, promises, storytelling, and mistruths.

Many of us become enclosed in our fears of the unknown. We are told what to fear, for example, through books, movies, and stories. Even people who are allowed to live authentically in their family and with friends meet resistance from people outside that community. They are perceived and labeled as being "weird," "strange," or "not normal." Some people say those who use their extrasensory abilities are "free spirits."

For many people, a life-changing event causes them to behave differently. It can happen through an event such as illness or accident or through situations of a spiritual nature, especially ones that cannot be explained in physical or scientific terms. We suddenly realize we are more than human beings. We begin to understand there is a connection between all of us, between nature and between the universe(s). We begin to return to our true state of being, as positive, loving, and nurturing spirits living a human experience. We suddenly remember what has been covered by the veil of forgetfulness when we journeyed through the birth as humans. This experience can be frightening or at least unsettling.

Some are meant to walk a journey of creative, unabashed expression and live a life on their own terms from the get-go. Others, like Barbara, experience a challenging life of stepping out of the comfortable enclosure of familiarity, experiencing the unknown, then returning to the former comfort zone. These people step out and step in, over and over, until the desire to share their gifts becomes more important than anything else in life. When the magic and the excitement of living life in divine purpose in the present moment, in balance between the physical and the spiritual, is discovered and embraced, life becomes enjoyable, even during the most challenging of experiences.

Yes, Barb is very much a star being. From Barb's experiences and her willingness to share them in a book, others will understand and believe they are loved beyond all measure. The masters who walk the earth at this time are praying and encouraging everyone to awaken to their understanding of the nuances and lessons of our experiences as humans. This is really helping to create more love on, and within, Mother Earth. This book serves as a platform for the ones beginning their journey, and a confirmation of those who are walking their path, on the journey to their heart. This autobiography is a testament that we are more than what we have been told and taught.

Chapter 1

MY OUT-OF-BODY EXPERIENCE

Until age thirty-one, I had been blessed with a relatively healthy body. I had the usual childhood illnesses—occasional colds and flu bugs. I didn't have weight issues or a desire to abuse alcohol or smoke tobacco. But one evening I sustained a serious injury that put me in the place of one of my critically injured patients.

In June of 1986, I met the man who would become my second husband, Hoyt L. Kesterson, II. He had wanted to date me for two years. When I ended a relationship with another man, Hoyt invited me over to his home for a swim in his pool and to watch a laser disc movie of my choice from his six-hundred-disc collection.

I drove over to his house and changed into my bathing suit in the guest bathroom. When I walked outside to the patio, I saw a crystal wine bucket and two wineglasses on the pool deck. My first thought was, *Wow, this is romantic, and I don't have any romantic feelings for this man.*

He asked me what wine I'd like, and I picked white zinfandel. We sat in the pool, on the steps, talking about life and sipping wine. After swimming, he gave me his terrycloth bathrobe to wear over my suit as we watched two movies in the living room. I noticed there were several cats walking around the house, checking me out. After the second movie, I got dressed and drove to my parents' house, where I had been pet-sitting their two cats while they were in California, picking up my sister from Stanford University for the summer break.

Hoyt called the next day and asked me out for dinner and a movie with a couple of his friends. I had never gone out to dinner with three men at the same time. But all three were friends of my family, and they worked in the computer business, so I accepted the invitation.

On the morning of the date, while taking my shower, I heard two loud bang sounds in my head. I didn't think nothing much of them. I felt delighted to share a dinner with three very brilliant men with golden hearts. We watched *Legal Eagles* and later ate at the Oscar Taylor restaurant at the Biltmore Fashion Park Mall in central Phoenix.

I offered to drive us in my new, seventeen-day-old gray Honda Accord. At the time, Hoyt drove a Yamaha 1100-cc motorcycle. On the way home, he asked me to drive on Missouri Avenue so he could stop at his bank's ATM to withdraw some money.

When we entered the intersection at Seventh Street, the last thing Hoyt said to me was, "You're a good driver. Oh, oh, she's coming through!"

A woman who had been drinking and was driving a large Oldsmobile sped through a red light and hit my car, just in front of the steering wheel. The strange sounds I had heard in the shower that morning were the sounds of that large Oldsmobile hitting my Honda Accord LX and causing it to fly through a chain-link fence. I hadn't realized that morning that I'd received a clairaudient premonition of the accident.

The driver of the Olds was angry at her husband, who had been driving. He had stopped the vehicle and gotten out. She had taken off, speeding through red lights, with her twelve-year-old daughter in the passenger seat. Just as she was traveling through the intersection, I looked to my left and saw her car in slow motion—coming toward me. Upon impact, my car went airborne, broke through the chain-link fence, and landed on a four-foot dirt mound at an excavation site on the corner.

When we landed, the thoughts running through my mind were, *I'm not finished. It's not my time to die. I'm here for my sister Valerie.* Hoyt, who wasn't wearing his seat belt, landed on the floor in front of his seat. He had upper and mid-back pain, and his right leg was hurting from hitting the dashboard. But he fared better than I did. Both of my lungs were collapsed because my collarbones were snapped in half. Hoyt's two-hundred-plus-pound body had flown across the car and into my one-hundred-eighteen-pound frame. Objects move in the opposite direction of force, and I just happened to be in his path. Five of my ribs were fractured on the right side. I also had glass in my eyes from the shattered windshield.

Luckily, this accident occurred in front of a fire station, so the emergency response time was almost immediate. People stopped their cars and rushed over to us. The paramedics pulled up in their fire trucks and saw how smashed up the cars were. The windshield was shattered, mostly on the driver's side, so it looked like I had hit it with my head.

"She's got a head injury!" the paramedic shouted when he saw red liquid dripping down my forehead, mistaking it for blood.

I reached up and pulled a strawberry off my head. "It's a strawberry. I didn't hit my head." My dessert, which had been in a Styrofoam container on the dashboard, was now all over the car. The photos taken by the accident investigator later showed what looked like lung tissue and blood in the interior of the car. But it was really cake, whipped cream, and smashed strawberries.

I could talk only in short sentences because it was hard for me to breathe—like breathing in the second dimension, without expansion. I knew I was in shock because I kept repeating, "He's allergic to penicillin, and I've got contact lenses in my eyes." I was afraid I was going to go unconscious and not be in control of the situation. I couldn't stop being a critical care nurse.

The paramedics told me to climb out of the vehicle myself and crawl onto the backboard. I was surprised they couldn't lift or help to lift my body out of the vehicle. I moved in excruciating pain from the broken bones touching the nerves as I exited the vehicle by myself.

As she strapped me down on the backboard on the ground, a female paramedic told me she would have to put a MAST suit on me because my blood pressure was low and for precautionary measures for shock. I remembered that the only people I saw in the ER with a MAST suit on were dead, and they had messed their pants. This was a message for me that I was in deep doo-doo.

But then the paramedic added, "We're not going to inflate the MAST suit; we just want to be prepared." This made me feel a little bit better.

It took the paramedics several attempts to start an IV in my arms. My large veins must have been closed down with adrenalin surging through my bloodstream to keep me conscious. We were loaded into an ambulance and taken to John C. Lincoln Hospital, where I had learned how to become an ER nurse eight years before.

It was estimated the other driver was traveling about sixty miles per hour at the moment of impact, due to the two-foot intrusion into my vehicle. She hadn't applied her brakes, which caused her to receive facial injuries, smashing her front teeth out on the steering wheel. Her daughter in the passenger seat sustained injuries to both knees from the dashboard impact. They were taken by ambulance to the same hospital.

The trauma team was waiting for our arrival. As soon as I was placed on the hospital gurney, the nurses cut away my favorite V-neck sweater top and my white cotton pants and undergarments. I was covered with a sheet and a warm, light blanket. The nurses placed a catheter into my bladder to monitor my urine output. My blood was drawn for lab tests and to check my alcohol level, which turned out to be zero, even though I had one Amaretto and cola with my meal.

When the trauma nurse attempted twice to put the stomach tube into my nose and down through my throat to suck out my dinner, my body rose up off the gurney and my nails sunk into the skin of her arm. My gag reflex was trying to keep the tube from going down. Finally, she was able to insert the tube on the third try.

Every time I moved my body, I felt unbearable pain. Trauma protocol dictates that doctors withhold pain drugs until they determine the extent of the injuries so narcotic effects don't cover up a life-threatening injury. Computerized tomography scans were taken of my abdomen to rule out internal injury. The pain from my broken ribs and collarbones shot down to my abdomen. After the doctor read the negative CT scan results, the trauma nurse took the stomach tube out.

The radiology tech burst through the ER doors, yelling, "She's got bilateral pneumos!"

The trauma nurse attending to me yelled back, "She's a nurse. She knows what you're talking about!"

I imagined she thought I would freak out. But I already knew I was in serious shape when the paramedic told her at my bedside that my respiratory rate was forty-four per minute. The norm is twelve to eighteen. That's when I understood there was a serious problem with my lungs. Being a critical care nurse, and because of my personality, I kept my cool and tried not to let on how nervous I was. I was scared that I might have a torn aorta that wasn't being picked up in the tests.

A trauma surgeon came to my bedside, introduced himself, and said I needed a chest tube to reinflate my right lung. I was diagnosed with a 50 percent hemorrhage and deflation of that lung. The left lung was collapsed about 10 percent and didn't require a chest tube. The nurses set up a sterile field for the procedure after the trauma surgeon performed his exam. He injected lidocaine into my right side to numb the skin. Then he made a small incision with a scalpel, where he injected the numbing medicine, blotted the blood away, then attempted to insert the tube. The chest tube is a semihard plastic tube with a metal spear inside, like a shish kebab skewer, with the diameter just larger than the size of a pencil. The skewer, better known as a trocar, has a sharp point to facilitate piercing through the muscle fascia.

The lidocaine did nothing for the pain. I was in so much pain, my muscles were tightened. The chest tube would not go in, and consequently my whole body was pushed across the gurney. This ignited my nerve fibers so much I began to scream obscenities at the top of my lungs. "Shit! Goddamn!" I couldn't hold the words back. At the same time I was yelling these cuss words, I was thinking Hoyt could hear me and he wouldn't want to go out with me again. But there was nothing I could do to stop screaming those words.

The trauma surgeon stepped back. The nurses readjusted me back on the gurney. He tried inserting the tube again, shoving me across the gurney. "Shit! Goddamn!" I grabbed my chest with my left hand, contaminating the sterile field. I screamed at the nurses, "Tie me down! I'm touching the sterile field!"

I could see in my third eye a list of the ten complications of a trocar chest tube insertion. I knew too much. I was very afraid the spear would slip and my heart, lung, liver, or spleen would be pierced like a piece of meat on a fork, and I would die. I was totally freaking out in the most excruciating pain and in the most intense fear I'd ever felt in my life. Gauging my level of pain, I promised God I would never complain about my menstrual cramps again.

On the third try, the tube was successfully inserted. The surgeon placed it deep inside to suck up the blood and the escaped air to allow my lung to reinflate over time. When this procedure was done, I was given a shot of Demerol for the pain.

Friends took Hoyt home, and I was admitted to the hospital intensive care unit. I received pain shots every four hours around the clock. Breathing treatments with a small nebulizer were given to me to prevent pneumonia and help my lungs reinflate. During one of these breathing treatments, I read my EKG monitor backward in my mirror on the overbed table and discovered my P-wave was missing. My heart was in a junctional rhythm. Although this wasn't life threatening, I felt the trauma surgeon should be aware of it. When the respiratory tech told the trauma doctor about the cardiac rhythm anomaly, the bronchodilator drug was discontinued.

On the third day, I was transferred to the telemetry unit for close observation. This is when I began reliving the accident. During these attacks, my heart rate jumped and my hands were wet with sweat. The nurses gave me pain medication for these events.

My parents came home during my fourth day in the hospital and got the message from my brothers that I was in intensive care. My mother broke down in tears. When they visited, my sister Maureen brought flowers and could see I was alive and well, considering the circumstances. On the fifth day, I was transferred to the regular floor. My bladder catheter was removed, but I still had the chest tube.

The day after the accident, Hoyt had to leave on a business trip in New England to defend the United States' position on a computer security protocol. This was a project he and his committee had been working on for two years. If he hadn't shown up, the United States would have lost the vote. He traveled in pain and was still able to perform his job.

Before he left, Hoyt sent me the largest bouquet of flowers I've ever seen a patient receive in a hospital. The nurses showed me them from the doorway, because flowers weren't allowed at the bedside in critical care units due to possible bugs transmitting diseases, and the limited shelf space for supplies and equipment.

The trauma surgeon removed my chest tube in the afternoon of the fifth day. My lungs had reinflated to 90 percent. If someone asks me if I know what a chest tube feels like with broken ribs, I can tell them. When you lie still and the tube isn't moved by anyone, at the point where the tube is inserted, and the surrounding two inches of skin, it feels like a blowtorch is under the surface. This sensation is constant. When the tube is moved, it feels like a knife is inside your heart, twisting back and forth. From this experience, I gained more empathy for people with chest trauma.

After a week in the hospital, I continued my healing in an electrical hospital bed at my parents' home for a month. I went back to work six weeks after the accident. I worked for two days with a shoulder muscle spasm. But when my right arm went numb and cold, I called the orthopedic surgeon assigned to my case and asked for four weeks of physical therapy. I made a complete recovery in ten weeks.

While recuperating, I noticed a part of my consciousness would separate from my mind and ask questions: *Why? Why are we here? Why are we having a conversation? Why is there a sofa? A chair? Why?* Everything appeared foreign to me. These episodes would occur when I was in conversation with people and when I was by myself, and they lasted for about one or two minutes. In the beginning this happened about five times a day. It scared me because I had no control over it. I wondered if I was going insane. I didn't realize I was having out-of-body experiences.

After several days, I decided to go with it. I would say in my mind, *Oh well, here we go again.* I no longer feared it. I figured it was what my mind had to do to cope with the trauma of a near-fatal accident. I didn't tell anyone about what I was going through.

These episodes gradually diminished in frequency and finally stopped after eight months. During this posttraumatic period, I didn't care if my bills were paid. I didn't care if I was on time for appointments. I was shocked at myself for feeling and behaving like this. At the time, my attitude was, *Hey, I'm not even supposed to be here.* And this perspective shocked me too. I just didn't care what people thought about me. Eventually, I became responsible again. I just figured this was how my mind dealt with the trauma.

Years later, two psychologists told me they had never heard of these types of experiences. When reading Joel Goldsmith's *The Art of Spiritual Healing*, I received a downloaded message that the portion of my consciousness that separated from me was my Higher Consciousness. Although it felt like a separation, it really wasn't. I was feeling the presence of my Higher Self. For brief moments, I pierced the veil of forgetfulness. My consciousness and awareness were being adjusted. For what, I didn't know at the time.

I was beginning to see my life changing directions. I started a relationship with Hoyt that turned into love. Within five months, he asked me to marry him. Actually, he first wanted me to move in with him. I said I would, if he agreed to marry me. After a fifteen-month courtship, we were married at the edge of the Grand Canyon in a small ceremony at Shoshone Point on September 5, 1987. It was filmed by a television company from London, Thames Television. As part of a travel show called *Wish You Were Here...?*, presented by the British actress Anneka Rice, our wedding was viewed by over thirteen million people in the United Kingdom.

Hoyt and I settled down to married life with travel and adventure. I worked at a small, local hospital part time in the emergency room, and he continued his computer standards work at Honeywell. During our eighteen-year marriage, we traveled to thirteen countries, and I was introduced to many cultures and customs. I am grateful for Hoyt giving me the world and the opportunity to begin my exploration of my spirituality.

Ten years later, at age forty-two, I began my conscious spiritual journey when I met my guardian angel.

Chapter 2

MEETING MY GUARDIAN ANGEL

I had stood in the emergency room nurses' station, reading the invitation flier taped to the mauve medicine cabinet door, above and next to the stainless-steel sink: "The angels are all around us. They're bright, beautiful beings of light who want to help us live a life filled with joy! In this one-and-a-half-hour seminar, you'll be guided to make the initial connection with your angels, and you'll learn how to work with them more directly for insight, guidance, healing, and inspiration. Let the angels lighten up your life!"[1]

This flier provided enough of a hook for me to want to attend. Besides, the cost was only fifteen dollars. I could afford that.

I thought back to my rigid parochial school days when Sister MaryEllen told the class to give names to our guardian angels. The nuns didn't guide us in a meditative state to communicate with our angels. Angels belonged in the Bible, with Mary and Jesus—at least, that's how I remembered it.

I wanted to believe, yet at the same time I doubted these entities were even real. Deep inside, I thought this playshop was too "New Age" for me. I even subscribed to a magazine for skeptics, for Pete's sake. *This is who I am*, I thought.

The other day while at work, I was feeling the dull, throbbing pain from my menstrual cramps. Gabriella, a fellow nurse from Queens, New

---

1   Ann Albers, "Meet Your Guardian Angel," playshop flier, 1997, www.visionsofheaven. com

York, offered to relieve the discomfort by performing a healing touch technique.

"Therapeutic touch is in the Nurse Practice Act, Barbara."

I had no idea what she was talking about. I didn't believe in this mumbo jumbo, so there was my chance to prove her wrong. "It's not going to work on me," I told her.

Gabriella was patient with me, which is strange for a New Yorker. "Just stand still," she said.

As she waved her hands around my pelvic area, in the front and back at the same time, in small spirals expanding outward, I announced, "It's not working. It's not working…It's working! It's working!" I was amazed. Within twenty seconds, my pain was gone.

Gabriella smiled and giggled. "I told you."

This was the first time I experienced what is known as energy medicine. Now my curiosity was nudged, and I thought, *Maybe this is what I need to step out of my ignorance and let myself be exposed to something outside of Western medicine.* After that energy healing demonstration, I felt I could trust it. I couldn't doubt that one because it worked on me.

It was Gabriella who offered to host the angel playshop in her home with angel communicator Ann Albers. Gabriella's spacious suburban home in the upscale Arrowhead neighborhood is two stories high. She decorated it with reproduction Native American artifacts that fit well with her belief in spiritual communications with the dead and animals. Gabriella has the ability to "read" a person just by tapping into the universal knowledge, much as a gifted virtuoso in music does.

Born and raised in Queens, Gabriella has the typical strong personality one finds in a New Yorker. When she voices her opinion, she prefers to tell it like it is—no fluff around the edges. This five-foot-two nurse and mother of a boy and girl raised her children while her husband worked in other states with the government (I don't remember exactly what he did). Their twenty-eight-year marriage ended in divorce, shattering Gabriella's happiness. She sought emotional and spiritual counseling with Ann.

"If it weren't for Ann, I don't know how I could have gotten through the anger and grief I felt when he left me." Gabriella has since transcended her grief and remains friends with her ex-husband.

As I entered the house, what looked like a grand staircase to me reminded me of entering a cathedral, drawing my eyes upward. The adjacent living room was void of furniture and had only beige carpet and four barren walls—a clean slate of space, without personality or style, the perfect place for fifteen women to sit on the floor and meditate. In the kitchen and family room, we gathered for the evening of meeting our angels, munching on snack-sized carrots, cucumbers, celery, and other culinary goodies. I felt separated from everyone, even though most of these women worked at the hospital too. I wanted to connect with some-one there, to share a common story or feeling of excitement about meet-ing an angel, but each woman I spoke to appeared to be just as nervous as I was.

Ann, a slender woman with shoulder-length hair, invited us to sit down in the living room. She looked like me: dark-brown hair, brown eyes, and a petite body. I wore jeans and a yellow cotton top with short sleeves, much like what the other women wore to be comfortable. Ann was an avionics engineer turned spiritual counselor who wore a floor-length navy-blue-and-turquoise dress with muted spiral shapes in a soft cotton fabric.

As we sat on the floor in an oval-shaped circle, all of us held hands for a few moments. Ann sat on a folding chair while giving a blessing invocation for this playshop. To introduce herself, she spoke about her career change from the corporate world to a course and lifestyle change of esoteric study with angels. She said that one day in a bookstore, she had asked God, *Is this all there is to my life?* At that moment, from a bookshelf against the wall, a book flew into the air and landed on the floor in front of her. Ann bent down, picked it up, and read it: *Ask Your Angels*, a book by Alma Daniel, Timothy Wyllie, and Andrew Ramer. She then left her corporate job and began apprenticeships with a psychologist, shamans, mystics, channels, mediums, and other spiritual teachers. She began giv-ing classes in angel communications and performed angel readings for people guided to come to her in a New Age store in Phoenix.

Giving her interpretation of angels—a different perspective from what I had known—Ann shared with us, "Angels are here to serve us; in serving us, they serve God. The angels, your angels, are right here. When we came to this planet, through the birth process, we had a veil placed over us, so we would forget who we are and where we came from in spirit, in order for us to live as a human being in this third-dimensional reality. Each of you has a guardian angel to watch over you and help you. The angels don't interfere in our lives or mess with our free will. Free will is a gift from God. On the other side of this veil is love. When we leave this third dimension, we go back into the love, or what we call the spirit world of existence. We never die."

As I heard these words and breathed a deep sigh of relief, my shoulders dropped about two inches. It was as if these were the words I longed to hear—like finding out your biopsy report is negative for malignancy. And yet I didn't understand why these words were so comforting.

What really tickled me was when Ann said, "Our angels have a sense of humor, just like us." I thought it was cool we could joke around with our angels because humor is an easy way to reduce stress. Humor places the angels on a more human level for closer communications between us and them.

Ann went on to explain about our extrasensory perceptions—like the "third eye" or "mind's eye"—the ability to see into the future and the past and to see symbols and messages. As I listened to her speak about spiritual concepts, I felt goose bumps and secretly I wondered, *Am I the only one feeling this way?* I looked around the room and saw others nodding their heads *yes* to the concepts Ann spoke about.

Ann went on. "When we close our eyes and relax, we can open our third eye and see visions of objects, places, people, even movies of these events. It takes practice for some people; others do this innately. And yet everyone has the ability to see through their third eye."

I told Ann I didn't talk with angels and added, "In my prayers, I speak directly with God."

She replied, "That's okay."

Calling in the angels for everyone's highest and greatest good, Ann helped us to connect and receive messages. For grounding purposes, she asked us to lie on the floor and get into a comfortable position. We closed our eyes and imagined an electrical extension cord protruding from the base of our spines, deep into the earth, to firmly "plant" us. We imagined another extension from the top of our heads, up into the heavens above, and then showering back around our bodies with sparkling glimmer lights.

Then we envisioned a rose-colored ball of swirling light just above our heads, slowly descending into our bodies, relaxing our scalps, foreheads, eyes, noses, ears, lips, skin, and muscles. As the ball of light sat momentarily at the base of my skull, I felt a warm, tingling sensation of relaxation shoot down my arms, into my hands and fingertips. The ball of light descended into my chest at the heart level, where it became enlarged with growing layers of light surrounding my entire body.

In a quiet tone, Ann encouraged us to ask our angels to reveal themselves. "Don't judge or expect the way your angel will contact you. Some of you will feel a touch, others a gentle breeze across your face, or perhaps you'll hear a quiet voice." After what seemed to be about ten minutes, Ann was guided to slowly bring us out of the meditation.

Each woman shared her experience with the group. Some felt a tingling sensation in one leg; others saw images of their angel with wings; still others heard their angel speak a greeting of acknowledgment. All of the other fourteen women experienced some form of communication with their angel, but not I. For me, it was a black void of outer space with no twinkling stars, nothing.

Ann nodded and said, "This is okay."

I wondered, *Should I ask for a refund? Why am I the only one in the room who didn't have an angel encounter? What's wrong with me? Why am I different?*

After a short break, we paired up and asked each other to obtain the answer to a question that began with the word *how.* I asked my partner, Brenda, "How can I meet my guardian angel?"

Brenda asked me, "How can I best help myself?"

When we returned to the meditative state, it was quicker this time. I knew what to expect in meditating, or maybe it was my body that knew what to expect. I was so relaxed I lay there with my mouth wide open.

Then I saw a vision. A burst of crimson light narrowed to become several of the wooden spokes of a solitary wagon wheel, rolling by on a dirt road in a late-summer straw-colored prairie. My view was at eye level with the dirt road, as if I were standing in a hole in the ground. I was amazed how this looked, as if I were watching a movie. The wheel moved from right to left, out of my vision.

After the meditation, I shared this image with Brenda, and Ann assisted in the interpretation of this message. "This is your path, Brenda," she said.

For me, Brenda saw a silver ladle dipping into a mountain spring. I remembered the lush green spring grotto on the pipeline hike I had taken in Milford Sound, New Zealand, years before. Someone had left a silver cup for any hiker to refresh themselves with a drink of cool glacier water.

Ann said, "You need to relax more to meet your angel, Barb. You are more of a feeler and a knower."

This encouraged me to share with her my premonitions, to share how I knew when someone was going to go into cardiac arrest in the intensive care unit where I worked as a critical care nurse. I also had a 100 percent track record as the education director in a local Phoenix hospital years before: I knew if a new nursing employee would stay employed or not. I knew this within five minutes of meeting him or her; this occurred during the two and a half years I held orientations every other week. I never disclosed this phenomenon to anyone because I didn't want anyone to think I was nuts, and I superstitiously wondered if sharing that information would jinx it. I didn't think of this as a psychic skill. I felt it was just good observation—nothing more.

Even though I had not met my guardian angel, I left the playshop feeling much better about angels and God. I felt a weight had been lifted off my shoulders in regard to what happens to people after death. Knowing other women came to the playshop and experienced their guardian angels helped me to understand I wasn't alone in wanting to meet *my* angel. I decided to practice the same meditation to meet my guardian angel the very next morning.

With my hands crossed over my heart, breathing deeply and slowly, I slipped into a deep meditation. With my husband still asleep on the other side of the king-size waterbed, the kind that doesn't make any motion when a person turns over, I continued breathing deeply and slowly. I felt enveloped by a loving, warm sensation, giving me encouragement. I was watching a movie through my third eye, yet still conscious in meditation and fully aware of my external surroundings. Barefoot, I walked on the soft emerald-green grass of the Arizona State Capitol Library. I didn't understand why I was drawn toward this building. Puffy white clouds in the blue sky slowly passed by. My right hand was hot and numb. The rest of my body felt normal. Almost as soon as I saw it, the library vanished. Everything vanished. The three-second movie was over.

My right hand turned cold. This was new territory for me. I didn't understand why my heart was racing. I didn't know if I could handle this. I slowly became aware of the rest of my physical body. It was time to get up and take my shower. I slowly moved the sheet off and stepped into my fuzzy pink slippers. I quietly walked out of the bedroom in my oversize pink T-shirt and then into the bathroom down the hallway. I preferred to use this bathroom because the sound of the shower didn't wake my husband.

Facing the mirror on the wall behind the double sinks, I pulled my T-shirt off. "What the…?"

There were five red burn-like marks on my upper right breast and four on the left. I touched the red skin. No pain. I placed my hands on my chest and saw my fingers matched up with the red markings. The image reminded me of a rising sun, with my fingers depicting the solar rays.

"What did this mean?" I knew I had followed the meditation instructions I'd learned the night before in the "Meet Your Guardian Angel" playshop with Ann Albers. "What was this?"

My heart pounding, I called Ann and told her about the red marks. With a gentle, motherly tone, she said, "Now, Barbara, you were the most skeptical person in the room that night. Some of us need physical evidence our angels are here. And Barbara, you are a healer. It is perfectly normal for the skin to become flushed under the fingers and hands of the healer. This is from the energy transfer. These skin blushes don't last very long and don't cause any pain." My shoulders dropped, and my heart returned to a normal pace. She was right; the marks vanished in an hour.

The following morning I attempted to meet my angel again. On my back in bed with my eyes closed, breathing deeply, I calmed myself into a relaxed state, just as I had in the meditation playshop. I stated my intention out loud: "I want to meet my guardian angel."

My third eye opened, and then I was watching a movie. Located in the forehead area, our third eye is the gateway to other realms of consciousness. I saw myself sitting on a lawn chair in the green grass next to a running creek. I saw an angel standing in the grass about five feet away. The sun's rays glimmered through the angel's soft, silky blonde hair, flowing over a pure white gathered ankle-length gown and large white feathered wings. The angel turned to each side, nose in the air, as if posing for a royal portrait. It had a Roman nose, yet its facial features did not reveal a gender. *This is my guardian angel?*

"You're a ham!" I said. This must be the humor Ann spoke about.

I asked in a fervent tone, "What is your name?" Gold flames in the form of capital letters with a medieval font appeared in midair, spelling the name *SOLARIUS*.

I was elated. My question had been answered! I thanked Solarius and slowly came out of my meditation. I did it! I was so happy finally to meet my guardian angel. I called Ann Albers and made an appointment for a one-hour angel reading session the following week.

Chapter 3

ANGELS AND MY AWAKENING

In October of 1997, upon entering Ann Albers's second-story apartment for my first angel reading, I noticed a white bookcase of spiritual books extending the length of the living room wall, from floor to ceiling—books about metaphysics, psychic skills, mediumship, prophecies, guides and angels, and more. I felt very excited when we sat down at a card table decorated with a purple crushed-velvet cloth and several crystals.

"These crystals of quartz and amethyst facilitate the connection and communication with our angels and guides," Ann assured me. Her voice was as happy and uplifting as her personality. I imagine she could feel my nervousness.

In this first angel reading, Ann and I held hands on the tabletop. With our eyes closed, she spoke an invocation to invite the angels and guides to share information with us during this reading.

"There are several guides helping you in your life. There is a man here, a bookkeeper named Jonathon, who worked near a boatyard in the late eighteen hundreds. He has a sweet, nice-looking face. His brown hair is soft and thick. He has long sideburns. This was the fashion of his day. He is very smart and thinks differently, using his lateral brain to find solutions by circumvention. He doesn't let anyone pull the wool over his eyes. He helps you in your business.

"There is a being who helps you in understanding how the human body functions. You use this knowledge in your healing work.

"There is a wise woman of advanced years who teaches you patience. She has long, silver hair and stands less than five foot three. Barbara, you lost your patience in a prior life because you died before you finished building an altar dedicated to the Blessed Virgin Mary in Southern France. You were the architect on that project, and you died from a terminal illness. You've carried this issue of impatience through many lifetimes.

"You also have a life-form that helps you find the truth. Another one assists you in replenishing your joy through relaxation. There is a green fairy here who assists in your connection to nature. This fairy loves egg-shaped objects."

My head began to ache with a pounding vibration inside. Ann gently asked the angels to step back a little so I could adjust to the high frequencies. The aching stopped. I inquired about my dad's recently deceased brother, my uncle Dave. Ann said he was unavailable at the time because he was in training to teach others to do better in life.

Ann saw that my aunts Betty and Irene (my mother's sisters) were also with me, especially when I cook and travel. She described Aunt Betty as someone who enjoys sitting in the car with her purse on her lap, taking in the scenery going by. Aunt Irene was described as being a quiet and demure woman, standing close to her sister. "They beam with happiness watching you in your everyday, normal activities, Barb.

You were an Egyptian healer who used massage oils in her work. In another lifetime, you were a woman in charge of a large harem. You made sure your girls were well cared for, and you used your womanly skills to manipulate men in business deals. You were savvy in politics and business matters."

I asked about my cat, Magic. "Magic is fine. There are no hard feelings here. Animals don't hold grudges like humans. They are loving and forgiving creatures." For years I had felt guilty for allowing my first husband, Jim, to give Magic to other people. This information helped me to forgive myself and to put this memory to rest.

I was fascinated I had help on the other side of what we know as our physical reality. I didn't understand how this worked, yet I found it intriguing. When I drove home, my eyesight was profoundly clear and sharp. I could see details in every object along the road. Cars, billboards, people, and dogs, close up and far away, were extremely sharp in appearance. It was as if I had the eyes of an owl or hawk. By the time I arrived home, this clear sight had changed back to my normal vision.

After learning about angels, guides, and loved ones who had crossed over—and that they are with me all the time—I began to feel different from how I'd felt before. It felt as if I were a stranger in a foreign city, without a road map or directions. In the evening before I went to sleep, I felt as if I were living in two worlds at the same time—the one I knew and the one I was stepping into. A feeling like this is like being pushed out onto a theater stage and being forced to perform in front of a huge audience when you don't even have these skills. It was scary! If these concepts of angels and guides were true, then why weren't my family and friends talking about them? Why do we keep these things secret? I felt fear for being aware of this information.

I decided to have an angel reading by Ann once every six months. I felt this was a good way of checking in on my spiritual journey's progress. I didn't feel I had to have someone hold my hand every step of the way or that I was going through a crisis. There must have been some part of me that was still skeptical because I found myself jumping out of my body during Ann's angel readings. Coupled with the excitement and fun of connecting with my guides and angels, I found it necessary to write my questions on a file card. It was so easy to get caught up in one track of questions and answers that I forgot to ask my other questions.

After Ann answered the first question on my card, she answered the second without me even asking. There was no way she could have seen my file card because I held it close to my body, and we sat opposite each other at her card table.

I started to interrupt her by telling her I hadn't asked the second question yet, but she said, "Wait, let's see how 'they' answer it. This could be fun."

Ann then said, "Because you are craving carbohydrates." My first question was not about food or health, so there was no hint what direction my questions were headed. My jaw dropped as I looked at my second question: "Why am I eating Cheerios in the morning and at night?" We both laughed.

For several years, I returned to Ann for angel readings and attended her workshops in communicating with angels and guides. I began reading books about angels and psychic communications and skills. I opened up more. After meeting my angel, I began hearing voices and seeing angels and scenes in my mind's eye. Sometimes before I saw something, I heard a sound.

For example, once I walked into my bedroom in the middle of the day after hearing the sound of a champagne cork popping. I asked my angels, "Are you all celebrating something?"

"Yes, at last, you acknowledged our presence. We are celebrating. Congratulations, Dear One." I could see a group of angels pouring sparkling wine and raising their fluted champagne glasses.

I wondered, *If angels are working behind the scenes in our lives, how often are we aware of their presence and their efforts? How often do we stop and appreciate all they do for us, in accordance with our free will, in serving God?* I felt I had a lot of thanking to do to catch up.

I was attracted to the angel books written by Doreen Virtue. She is a clairvoyant psychotherapist who gives workshops on spiritual psychological issues and conducts a practitioner program creating angel therapists. In *Healing with the Angels*, Doreen says, "The angels are here to teach us that God's love answers all questions and challenges. Our angels love us unconditionally, and they will never leave us while we are here on Earth."[2] This means no matter how much and how many times I screw up, I am still loved. This must also apply to everyone on the planet. Doreen helped me to open my heart to understanding how angels work and the various ways we can communicate with them. Through affirmations, prayers, love, and gratitude, we open the lines of communication for their help to reach us.

My angels were not sitting around getting drunk on sparkling wine just because I finally acknowledged their presence of forty-two years. This was their way of communicating their happiness. It was a gentle and fun way to help me understand how communication works with them. Yet I later found out that this isn't the only way they transmit messages.

I had to unlearn what I had been taught and how I had created myself into being a super-organized, anal-retentive, egotistical critical care nurse. For me, it was black or white—no gray areas allowed. I was rigid and skeptical in my thinking and in my behavior with people. I had to be in control. At the same time, I must have been this way for a purpose. It's not that it was a bad way to behave. I just didn't know better. I have heard that some people believe we are programmed from birth to act as we do. Perhaps it was protective for me until I awakened to my spiritual awareness. Maybe I wanted to experience life as I knew it and then later open to a different awareness.

2   Doreen Virtue, PH.D, *Healing with the Angels*, Hay House, p.1–2

I began to explore the sixth senses and began having experiences with each one. I had even experienced an encounter with my Higher Self twenty-some years earlier, but didn't know it.

My very first clairaudient message from my Higher Self occurred in November of 1976. Returning from a Christmas shopping trip in Mexico, my Catholic boyfriend at the time and I stopped at the seventeenth-century Tumacácori Mission eighteen miles north of Nogales. While I was standing next to the water fountain, I heard a voice just above my head and to the right: *"He's going to leave you."*

I looked around and didn't see anybody near me. The voice's volume was as if someone had stood behind me, and the tone was without emotion, very matter-of-fact. When I got back in my boyfriend's truck, the words haunted me. At the same time, it felt as if I were preparing myself for a future event.

That Christmas Eve, after we exchanged gifts, my boyfriend announced, "I'm breaking up with you. Good-bye." And he drove away. I felt devastated that he would break up with me during a joyous time of year. I cried for four days, and then I moved on with my life.

Clairaudience is the ability to hear in a paranormal manner, and the guidance is always positive. Our angels are not going to tell us to harm ourselves or others. One morning, as I left my car in a shopping mall parking lot on the way to a shop specializing in award mementos, I heard a voice just above my head: *"They screwed it up."*

I said to the voice, "Okay."

As the incoming chapter president of a national legal nurse consultant organization, I had ordered a custom appreciation plaque for the outgoing president of our chapter. After receiving this message, I felt more prepared to check the work before I paid the bill. This information also lowered my stress level. I had placed the order several weeks before the plaque was to be presented at the next chapter meeting, giving time for mistakes to be fixed. Sure enough, I was handed the plaque by the store employee and saw the word *nurse* missing from the title. I didn't become upset. I just pointed out the error and asked if I could pick up the corrected plaque the following week.

That situation was pleasant, and the plaque mistake was not a waste of my time and effort. To me, this was an opportunity for my Higher Self to demonstrate the benefit of clairaudience in my day-to-day activities.

Clairvoyance is the psychic ability to see beyond the power of natural vision. This vision can occur as miniature movies, stationary objects, people, animals, and so on, inside or outside a person's head. An example of clairvoyance occurred one day at lunch. My husband asked me if I knew what happened the night before, around midnight.

I said, "Our next-door neighbor's garage door was wide open."

My husband exclaimed, "How did you know? You were asleep."

"When you asked me the question, I saw the neighbor's garage door open, and it was dark outside."

Several years after I had changed my career to legal nurse consulting, I tested my clairvoyance with a cooperative female coworker at the insurance company where I worked at the time. She was intrigued with my experiment. I asked her to write down a question on a file card. I told her to write it at any time she chose. We agreed to meet at the end of the week. A couple of days later, I sat at my desk and opened my third eye and wrote down what I saw and heard, though none of it made sense to me.

At the end of the week, I answered her question before she asked it. In addition, I shared with her another situation I saw in a vision: a man, a tire blowing out, and a jail. A month later, she shared with me her ex-husband was involved in a high-speed chase with the police and his car's tire blew out. He was apprehended and went to jail.

Claircognizance is the ability to know an answer or information about people, questions, objects, and so on. Psychic experts call this ability "clear knowing." Premonition is a form of claircognizance.

Back in the early 1980s, while working the night shift in the intensive care unit, I felt something. I announced to my coworkers, "What if we had two codes happen at the same time? Could we handle the situation?" Usually codes were a single event involving only one patient going into cardiopulmonary arrest and requiring resuscitation. The one emergency room physician is summoned to the bedside to direct the code team of nurses and respiratory technicians. There was a single crash cart in the unit, filled with resuscitation equipment and drugs that we used at the bedside.

Later that night, two patients went into cardiopulmonary arrest at the same time. The ER doctor came to the intensive care unit, and we nurses successfully resuscitated those patients. The charge nurse asked me, "How did you know?"

I replied, "I don't know. The thought just came into my head."

Naturally, one could easily assume this premonition was a fluke, unless it happened again. And it did, the following week. I repeated the same announcement, followed by a double code. To the best of my recollection, these patients were resuscitated, only to remain in comas and succumb to their illnesses.

I wasn't involved in the care of these patients, and my fellow nurses never mentioned the events or asked me to predict future ones. I wondered why these two premonitions of two double codes during twenty-two years of my bedside nursing career had occurred. Many other patients coded—granted, not at the same time—as these patients had. Could it be because I was working the night shift with nurses who did astral traveling and were spiritually open? I shared these stories with Ann Albers after the Guardian Angel playshop. She said I was sensing the energy from these events, even before they occurred. Ann said further, "Think of it as the isoelectric line of an oscilloscope where you have a straight even horizontal signal. When these events occur, the energy spikes the signal upward. That spike is what you are feeling." I enjoyed working with these nurses and learned more than I was taught in nursing school. Yet my psychic skills were not spoken about, at least not to me. Before I met Ann Albers, I was claircognizant and didn't know it.

One day, when I looked at my face in the nurses' lounge mirror, the knowledge that one of our patients would require resuscitation soon came into my mind. I was even receiving premonitions of people who were coding in the ER, knowing the resuscitated patient would soon arrive in the intensive care unit. Sometimes this premonition would occur as I focused while documenting my notes in my patient's chart.

Another time, I experienced confirmation of my claircognizance. A friend of mine whose fiancé died in a plane accident delivering blood to an Indian reservation in Arizona was excited when I came up to her in the parking lot outside the funeral chapel. "I want to tell you after the service what happened last night, Barbara."

When a mutual friend told me about this man's tragic death, I wanted to make something for the family to eat. They would be arriving in town from other states and would need nourishment during this gathering to grieve this man's passing and celebrate his life. I thought for a moment about what would be tasty and good to eat. Deviled eggs came to mind, so I prepared the eggs and took them over to the house. I figured they could eat the eggs for a snack in the evening.

My friend told me that when the deviled eggs were passed around, the floor lamp next to the deceased man's favorite recliner in the living room was off. Then the lamp light came on and off three times by itself. Those who witnessed this felt his presence and his approval. Deviled eggs were his favorite. This is an example of me receiving a message from beyond this physical reality and helping to comfort and "deliver" a message to a grieving family from their loved one who had crossed over and was very much with them and happy.

In the beginning of my spiritual awakening, I experienced my clairsentience in a frightening manner. Clairsentience is the ability to pick up another's emotions or physical sensations as if they were your own. Without a spiritual teacher guiding me about grounding and protection, I walked straight into a situation involving negative energy. I was given a warning, but I didn't heed it.

During an angel reading with Ann in 1998, I had asked my angels if the house next door was energetically clean—meaning the energy of the home was positive and happy. Ann replied, "No, put up a fence of white light, and you will be fine."

I soon discovered why the home was not clean and what can happen to us when we don't protect ourselves from negative energies, especially when we are clairsentient.

My neighbor, Debbie, and I had begun talking about angels and metaphysical concepts during our back-porch teas. We would sit for hours, smelling the sweet star jasmine growing up the porch post and watching my cats frolic on the grass, chasing butterflies and birds. She shared her views on organic vegetarian cooking and natural homeopathic medicine. I see so much of myself in her—her dark hair, slender body, and independent nature as a businesswoman. She is a very smart and down-to-earth individual with the most tender personality.

One day she asked me to come over and see if I felt something weird in one of the bedrooms in her house. Of course, I was curious and wanted to help her. When I walked into the front corner bedroom, I became nauseated and cold. The longer I stood in the middle of the room, the more I became dizzy and full of fear. With my heart racing and my mind feeling like it was going in a thousand directions at the same time, I told Debbie this was not a pleasant feeling at all. I felt the same in the other bedroom, but not to the same degree. Debbie felt something, too, but didn't understand why. She knew something wasn't right. I shared with her that, years before, the family who lived there had two little boys, and the mother was very controlling of them and unsociable to me.

Since I was feeling ill, I told Debbie I was going home and would call my friend Gabriella, who could help people in such situations. Gabriella considers herself a white witch and clairvoyant—possessing the tools to clear homes and buildings. I ran home and spoke in a shaky voice on the phone with Gabriella.

She told me, "You must get into a warm bath with sea salts immediately. Tell your friend to sprinkle sea salt on the ground in front of the doors and on the windowsills. I will come over tomorrow to check the house and clean it. Stay close to your husband; he has a protective blue light around him."

I told her, "Okay, thank you, Gabriella."

As I soaked in the tub, my husband came into the bathroom and asked if I wanted to go to the movies. "Sure!" I replied, without hesitation.

As soon as we sat down in the theater, I could not stay in my seat. With my husband seated to my left, I propped my right leg over his right leg and wrapped my arm around his shoulder, as if I were trying to sit on his lap. Even in a darkened movie theater, it felt strange to be covering my husband's lap like a blanket, but I couldn't stop the powerful urge to feel safe.

After about twenty minutes, I finally felt grounded enough to sit back. Sinking back into my seat, in my mind, I said to my guardian angel, *"I'm so sorry for jeopardizing my sanity."*

I heard a voice in my head say to me, *"You did no harm, Dear One. This was an experience you wanted to have so you can help others."*

I felt relieved I hadn't done permanent damage to myself, and I returned to watching the movie, feeling like my normal self.

The next day, Gabriella and I went over to Debbie's home. Even though its Southwestern stucco has white paint, the house looked dark to Gabriella. As we approached the front door, she advised me to place blue light all around my body for protection.

Debbie was glad to see us. When we entered the bedroom, both Debbie and I felt intense sensations. We didn't experience untoward effects in our bodies because we had protected ourselves beforehand.

Gabriella explained, "In this bedroom closet—this is where the children went to hide in fear of their father. These boys were abused. The energy of fear is still here and in the walls." She burned sage in the rooms and instructed Debbie to burn a white candle in the middle of each room for twenty-four hours, with the intention of clearing the rooms of negative energies.

We sat down in the living room, where Debbie showed us the fireplace and the shoe print depressions in front of it. These depressions, the size of a man's foot, showed that someone had walked from the front of the hearth over to the acrylic painting on the left side of the fireplace. Every time Debbie tried to vacuum the carpet to remove the impressions, they reappeared within an hour.

Gabriella stood in front of the painting with her eyes closed and her right hand gently touching it. "The artist wants us to know he is here, in the house," she said, "protecting Debbie and her husband from the negative energies present." The painter was Debbie's brother-in-law, who had died years before. My body tingled all over in confirmation.

After this situation, Debbie and her husband remodeled the home, tearing down and replacing the drywall and decorating the home with new wood flooring, tile, paint, and decor, expressing their creative style and joy.

When Gabriella drove over to my house for a visit the following week, she said, "That house is much brighter."

This was my first experience with this type of paranormal phenomena. I have since learned a medium and tarot card reader Victoria Gross notes that negative thought forms are residual mental or emotional debris in an environment. Negative thought forms can occur where excessive drug, alcohol, or physical abuse transpired.[3]

I'm grateful to Gabriella for sharing her knowledge of these metaphysical matters with me. She taught me more about protecting myself, candle ceremonies, using our other senses to see into the future and situations, working with crystals, and communicating with our guides and angels. She provided a safe environment for me to begin exploring the skills and knowledge that lay dormant within me. She didn't judge me or tell me I was crazy.

* * *

In the beginning of my awakening, I also began receiving deep-tissue massages from Nani, a massage therapist and Reiki practitioner. Nani is a petite, naturally tan woman from Hawaii. When I met her, she told me her age, but I didn't believe it. She looked years younger, and her hands

---

3   [1] Victoria Gross, "What Are Ghosts?", World of the Unknown, http://www.worldoftheunknown.com/articleGhost.html.

and arms were strong. Because she did house calls, I made an appointment for her to come to my house and set up the master bedroom for the massage. I cut a Sutter's Gold rose from the garden, stuck it in a bud vase with water, and placed it on the dresser. I also put on a relaxing music CD.

When I opened the front door in my bathrobe and slippers, I found a brown-haired woman holding a massage table folded in half inside a carrying case. She spoke with a soft voice and radiated a kind and compassionate feeling. After Nani prepared the massage table, I laid down and covered my naked body with the flannel sheet. With the soft music playing in the background, Nani began massaging my back. She found my muscles were so tight, she had to use her elbow and all 120 pounds of her body to move my tissues. I had bruises all over my back the next day. I didn't mind. I had heard a therapeutic massage is more intense than a soft "feel good" massage anyway.

Nani explained how we keep our issues in our tissues. "And man, you have a lot of issues, Barb," she said.

I replied, "Okay, then let's do it again in a couple of weeks." I began to offer Nani the rose, but during the massage, the rose had gradually gone limp.

Nani said, "Oh no, I want the rose!"

"Nani, it looks awful."

"That's okay. I still want it."

I handed the toxin-filled rose to her.

A couple of days later, Nani called and told me what had happened to the rose, which she had experimented with at home. She put the rose in a vase with water and placed it on the kitchen table. She held her hands around it and performed a healing called Reiki. Within five minutes, the rose bloom began to move upward until it was facing the ceiling again.

Nani began giving me massages about every two to three weeks. She taught me about spiritual concepts and was able to give me insights about myself. She could read me like a book, and she wouldn't hold back. I liked Nani's honesty with me, even if I didn't want to hear it. I learned to trust in hearing the truth, because this is where we grow spiritually and emotionally. Nani eventually became a Reiki master.

As I opened more of myself to the metaphysical realm, I continued to experience a great deal of fear and questioning of myself. I could not talk to my husband about these matters at the time; he just rolled his eyes. I was so afraid he would have me locked up in a psychiatric facility—or worse, leave me. I certainly couldn't talk to my family about this; after all, I was brought up Catholic, and these concepts did not fit into the teachings of the church. I sensed my family felt uncomfortable about these subjects. I was living in two worlds.

When my mother asked me why I was learning about metaphysical subjects, I told her, "I want to improve myself. I want to be a more compassionate and loving person." My mother replied, "You are already loving." From her response, I sensed she didn't understand me. I couldn't expect her to understand; this was new to me too. I had to learn about allowing others to be who they are, even if it doesn't make sense to me.

I didn't know how I could become more loving and compassionate; I just wanted to be. I felt I had to start walking this journey, no matter how difficult and how much I stumbled. I no longer enjoyed gossiping and complaining about situations and people. I began to ask, *What is my reality?* At night, I asked myself, *Why am I here?* and I would experience a sickening intense fear before I went to sleep. Each morning I woke up feeling better. But how and why? Was something happening in my dream state that removed my fears, only for them to build up again during my daily experiences and questions? I couldn't let this fear get the best of me.

I kept on walking the path, becoming more energized and happy about developing my extrasensory skills. Eventually the fear lessened as I became more comfortable in understanding metaphysics and focusing on the love and joy of being in a compassionate and forgiving frequency.

I continued giving myself more experiences. Psychometry, the ability to scan an object mentally to find out its history, vibration, or message, is related to clairsentience. A coworker asked me to perform "readings" on the jewelry she wore to work. A bracelet with stones was helping her to connect with her loved ones who had crossed over. Other jewelry assisted her in loving herself.

I tried this psychometry skill at the insurance company where I worked. There was a file of two male college students involved in a fatal auto accident. They were ejected from their vehicle, which rolled several times, in a "road rage" situation. Both men died at the scene from massive internal injuries. Usually lawyers don't submit photographs of deceased individuals in accidents, but sometimes it's done to shock the insurance adjuster into settling the bodily injury/wrongful death claim quickly.

I performed a psychometric reading on the photograph of one of the men. Sitting at the desk, I closed my eyes with my right hand over the picture. I asked my guides, *"What did this man feel at the moment he crossed over into spirit?"*

Even though I had protected and grounded myself that morning, immediately my mind went into a thousand different directions at the same time. It felt like insanity and confusion with an enormous amount of fear. This man's fear of impending death became mine. My heart rate jumped up to about 180 beats per minute, and sweat poured down my forehead. My hands were wet with nervous fear.

Now that I had accessed this information, I didn't know how to step away from it. I opened my eyes, closed the file, and said to myself, *Oh, oh, I can't go back to work like this. What am I going to do? I can't even think straight.* I sat back in the chair and placed my palms up in the air, closed my eyes again, and prayed, *"Mother Mary, would you please give me a healing to remove this situation from my mind?"*

The Blessed Virgin's open hand appeared in the air above my head, with fingertips down. Healing salt began pouring from her palm, showering all over me. My mind and heart rate instantly returned to normal, and the sweating stopped. I returned to my other work, wondering how I knew to ask Mother Mary for help. I've heard it said the answers are within us. This experience was a demonstration of that truth.

This type of psychometry was a bit too advanced for me at the time. I hadn't fully embraced the importance of protecting myself before accessing this type of information. I still walked into situations without protection. I'm grateful I knew to call on the Blessed Mother for assistance. I don't recommend engaging in this type of psychometry to people not skilled in it, unless someone who has developed psychic skills is there to assist. The message I hear is that our Ascended Masters, such as Jesus Christ, Quan Yin, and Mary, as well as the archangels, are here within us to help when we need it most. When we are in a state of profound sincerity and contrition, we will be blessed and saved by God and our guides. This was my proof of this help.

Chapter 4

THE BEGINNING OF MY HEALING

In early October of 1998, I came home from working in the emergency room and announced to my husband, "I'm going to work in an insurance company."

He protested, "No, you can't quit your job at the hospital."

A couple of days later, I blurted out again, "I'm going to work in an insurance company."

These statements were unsettling to my husband, and he asked, "How do you know this information?"

"I don't know. I just know." I was starting to sound strange to myself.

Later that week, on a Friday, I found a job advertisement in *The Arizona Republic* newspaper for a medical-claim review nurse at a large insurance company in Phoenix. On Saturday, I attended a job fair and introduced myself to the recruiter at the insurance company booth. I handed my résumé to the recruiter and told her I was interested in working for the company. The following Monday I received an invitation for a job interview. And after the interview, I received and accepted the job offer. This was my exit out of bedside nursing in a hospital.

In 1993, my seasonal allergies worsened to the point where I was ingesting diphenhydramine to keep my nasal passages open. I drank caffeinated beverages to counteract the drowsiness from the antihistamine. I went to an asthma and allergy clinic in Glendale, Arizona, for allergy testing in the spring of 1994. The pulmonologist tested me for various allergens and determined allergy shots would be beneficial. I received these injections every two weeks in his shot clinic until 1999.

On January 15, 1999, about ten seconds after receiving a routine injection in the allergy office, I became hot and anxious. My heart pounded rapidly. I told the nurse that something was happening inside my body from the injection. She took me into one of the treatment rooms, and I was given medication to counter the effects of the allergy shot. Oxygen was administered. I received a shot of epinephrine (adrenalin) in my arm and was given a diphenhydramine tablet to swallow. After about forty-five minutes, the symptoms subsided, and I was released to go home.

When I got to my car in the parking lot, I had another "reaction." I felt very scared. I wasn't sure if I was going to pass out in my car and die quietly from anaphylactic shock. The allergy clinic was closed by then, so I decided to just sit in my car. When I felt well enough, I drove over to my parents' house for a planned dinner. When I got there, my mother said my eyes looked like death. I lay down on their living room recliner in an altered state of consciousness. I was still feeling the effects of the epinephrine. I had stomach pain, shivering, nausea, general aches, and anxiety. My whole body shook like an earthquake. My parents left me alone and ate their dinner. Then just as suddenly as it had started, the symptoms disappeared. I ate a small meal and went home two and a half hours later.

Twenty-five hours after the initial reaction in the shot clinic, I had another reaction while sitting on the sofa watching television. It was as if someone had lit me on fire. I immediately sensed my whole body was hot, and my heart rate was around 180 beats per minute. This time, I ran to the bathroom and looked in the mirror. All of my skin was bright red, and my whole face was swollen. I felt this was an allergic reaction, so I called my neighbor to take me to the emergency room two miles away. She jumped in her car and came over to pick me up.

We arrived at the hospital, where four ambulances were lined up, delivering patients into the emergency room. I walked past the ambulances and to the nurses' station. "I'm having an allergic reaction," I exclaimed, "and I need drugs now!"

The emergency room was packed with patients, and the nurses were very busy. These compassionate nurses, my prior fellow coworkers, placed me in a recliner near the nurses' station and took care of me. They administered the epinephrine and diphenhydramine to counteract the allergic response. The ER doctor diagnosed urticaria and prescribed hydroxyzine hydrochloride, a first-generation antihistamine that is also used for anxiety and tension.

Urticaria occurs when the immune response causes mast cells to release histamine in an allergic reaction. A release of chemicals, including the histamine, causes a very irritating itching sensation. Swelling of the skin comes from fluid leaking out of the cells. While there may be a variety of symptoms a person can experience, I had no welts on my skin. My skin turned bright red. My breathing became labored with grunting exhalations. My heart pounded rapidly, and my blood pressure soared to over 200/110. On top of these symptoms, I had anxiety. Although I have been trained to handle and understand life-threatening medical conditions, the anxiety experienced during these episodes was very difficult, if not impossible, to control. I literally felt I was going to die.

For the next two weeks, I experienced these symptoms at all times of the day. I would wake up at midnight drenched in my sweat, anxious, breathing rapidly, with my heart beating like crazy. I had no control over what I was feeling in my body. I knew I wouldn't die, yet I couldn't convince myself. I had not learned how to give up control. I took an antihistamine pill every time these episodes occurred, until they eventually dissipated.

I returned to the allergy clinic, where my doctor prescribed another antihistamine called cetirizine, a nondrowsy formula to take in the morning. I took the hydroxyzine hydrochloride only at night because it also promoted sleep. With the combination of these drugs, I felt completely normal. I no longer took allergy shots, because these oral medications controlled my seasonal allergies too. I complied with this medical treatment to the letter.

* * *

My friend Gabriella asked if I was interested in receiving the First Degree Reiki attunement. After learning that Reiki is a natural healing method from Japan that anyone can perform, I agreed. During a two-day weekend course with Reiki master Ann Albers, I learned about the universal energy life force that flows through every human, plant, and animal. There's a technique to use this energy life force to promote balance, healing, oneness, and consciousness. I learned with Reiki that we can help ourselves and others grow spiritually, boost and balance our immune system, heal ourselves and others, and more. Since Reiki is not based on one particular belief system, it was okay with me. It didn't matter if I was

Catholic or any other faith—it just works. As a nurse I enjoyed helping people to heal and feel better through Western medicine modalities. Now I was open to try a different healing technique.

There are three levels in the original Usui Reiki tradition: Level I, Level II, and Master Level. Level I is a class where explanations and the initiations are given. Level II is another course where a person learns to send Reiki long distance. The Master Level course prepares the student to become a teacher of Reiki and initiate others who want to share Reiki healing with loved ones, friends, animals, and plants. It was recommended to me that a person wait three to five years between Level II and the Master Level, as the Reiki energy becomes stronger over time. The Master student is also given the course material to teach Reiki classes.

On the first day, we learned how to give ourselves a Reiki treatment. I liked the fact you don't need to be in a certain room or wear special clothing. After receiving the first attunement, the energy in my body became elevated. It felt like I was stepping through a light fog into more clarity. I was cautioned that my life as I knew it would change. What I didn't realize was how much. On the way home from class, I saw a strange gray ring around birds flying in the distance. I shared this with Gabriella, who was driving us home. She explained that these are the auras around birds. I also noticed this energy ring around planes, helicopters, and other flying objects with humans on board. Eventually, I began to see colors in the sky around trees and mountain ranges. Since receiving Reiki attunements, I see twinkling, orbiting lights in the air all around me. I learned this is the orgone, or chi, in our environment. I also see what looks like snow falling outdoors, even in our desert climate on hot summer days. It's not harmful to us. Rather, it's life-sustaining energy for us, animals, and plants.

On the second day of the Reiki course, I learned how to give another person an energy healing. This student and I lay on Reiki massage tables, listening to soft synthesizer music, feeling the warm waves of healing through our bodies. I melted like an ice cube in the summer sun. The additional attunements we received produced a higher energy level in our bodies.

The following evening, while watching television by myself, a strange event occurred in the living room. At the time, our cat Sasha was lying on my lap. Hoyt was in California on a business trip. Suddenly, the whole living room began to vibrate. It was as if the room were electrically charged. One of the other cats, a black-and-white male tabby named Mr. Mom, was spooked. He ran through the living room and jumped up on the brick planter. He was wildly looking back and forth, crying in a loud, shrill voice, as if he were seeing something or someone.

Sasha jumped down onto the wood floor as I got up. I walked around the back of the sofa, feeling dizzy and nauseated, and opened the back French door. Sasha ran outside. I called to Mr. Mom to run outside because I sensed he would be more comfortable outdoors, where he could run if he had to. He ran by me like a streak of lightning. I sat back down on the sofa, and my body vibrated. I went into an altered state of consciousness, with my heart racing. I didn't understand what was happening to me and what was causing everything, including the air in the living room, to vibrate too. This vibration lasted for about twenty minutes.

I picked up the portable phone and called Ann. After telling her how this scared the crap out of me, she calmed me, saying, "One of your angels decided to step into your body. All you have to do is remind your angels you are still human and not ready for this type of experience yet." My senses returned to normal. I was no longer nauseated or dizzy.

After I received first-degree Reiki, people began to perceive me in a different way. They sensed something about me had changed, but they couldn't figure it out. Some said I appeared happier. I had been cautioned that people might not see me and physically run into me. While shopping at a department store in Phoenix, a woman literally ran into me in the women's clothing section. "I'm sorry, I didn't see you," she said.

I replied with a smile, "It's okay. I understand." It happened just as Ann had said it would.

When I gave Hoyt a Reiki treatment, he fell asleep within minutes of a session. All four of our cats enjoyed receiving Reiki treatments too. I could tell by the sound of their contented purr.

Shortly after I received the first-degree Reiki attunement, an insurance adjuster at work who didn't like me suddenly changed his attitude toward me. He said to me, "Barb, your work is the best I've ever seen. I really appreciate your contribution, and you are really helping me to understand the medical issues."

Inside I was stunned. From that day forward, we collaborated and had fun discussing our work. I actually looked forward to performing reviews for him. We got to know each other's family stories. The day he retired, I cried. My heart still opens up when I remember him. What I learned from this is, even though you might not get along with someone, it could change later for the better. Anything is possible. Perhaps, through Reiki, and allowing more love to flow through my body and energy systems, I allowed more love to flow from a fellow human being to me.

After eight months of antihistamine treatment, I asked my doctor about stopping the medicines. He told me I could try a trial period without the antihistamines, but I probably would not be able to tolerate the symptoms after three days. In the evening of the second day, while sitting in an insurance adjuster certification class, I began to experience anxiety. It crept up slowly, and by the time I had walked downstairs to my car at the end of class, I was in a full-blown reaction. I didn't tell anyone what was happening to me; the parking lot was empty, and it was dark outside. With the blood pressure meter and stethoscope in my car, I discovered my blood pressure was very high and my heart was racing. I called Hoyt and told him my predicament: I couldn't concentrate enough to drive myself home. I sat in the dark parking lot by myself, trying to keep a grip on my sanity, while I waited for him to come pick me up. I spent the next two days at home, taking the medicine and waiting for the antihistamine to rise to a therapeutic level. Disappointed with my body, I continued taking the drugs. I still wanted to be free from the antihistamines, but I didn't know how to do this by myself. What bothered me the most was I imagined if I were stuck someplace, traveling to another country and running out of the medicine. What would I do? I hated being dependent on a drug just to feel normal. Two years later, the desire to find a cure for this affliction led me to a form of energy treatment called Jin Shin Jyutsu.

Chapter 5

JIN SHIN JYUTSU HEALING

In the summer of 2001, Hoyt and I went on a vacation in his Miata to Oregon. We traveled US 1 along the coast from Los Angeles to Ashland. It was fun riding in a convertible with our clothes stuffed in tote bags stored in the breadbox-size trunk and staying in budget hotels. We did this trip four times in the same number of years. We met the Arizona Theatre Company Shakespeare tour up there and saw plays at night in the reproduction open-air Globe Theatre, modeled after the original in London, England. On this last trip, I flew home while Hoyt took his time and drove the Miata back to Phoenix.

When I opened the mail at home and saw Ann's newsletter, I found a small advertisement for Jin Shin Jyutsu offered by Elizabeth Kuester. Elizabeth is a certified nurse practitioner, Reiki master, and Jin Shin Jyutsu practitioner. Something inside me knew this form of treatment would be a cure for my urticaria. I just plain knew it.

I called Elizabeth and asked her, "Have you treated urticaria before?"

She said, "No, but I'm willing to help you with this condition. I have seen other metabolic problems cured with Jin Shin Jyutsu."

I told her, "Your form of treatment will cure my urticaria." We agreed to meet at her office on the following Saturday afternoon.

Jin Shin Jyutsu physio-philosophy is an ancient art of harmonizing the life energy in the body. This form of treatment was passed by word of mouth from generation to generation. In the early 1900s, Master Jiro

Murai in Japan cleared himself of a life-threatening illness through Jin Shin Jyutsu. He devoted the rest of his life to the research and development of this form of healing. He collected his experiences and resources, including the *Kojiki* ("Record of Ancient Matters"). Eventually Jin Shin Jyutsu was given to Mary Burmeister, who brought it to the United States in the 1950s. Her school is in Scottsdale, Arizona.

Jin Shin Jyutsu employs twenty-six "safety energy locks" along energy pathways, called meridians, that feed life into our bodies. When one or more of the paths become blocked, the resulting stagnation can disrupt the local area and eventually block the complete path of energy flow. Holding these energy locks in combination can bring balance to the mind, body, and spirit, thus promoting healing.

This treatment can be applied as self-help or by a trained practitioner. The sessions generally last about an hour, and they don't involve massage, manipulation of muscles, drugs, or any other substance. It is a gentle art practiced by placing the fingertips (over clothing) on designated safety energy locks to harmonize and restore the energy flow. This facilitates the reduction of tension and stress that accumulate through normal daily living.[4]

On July 21, 2001, I met Elizabeth for my first one-hour healing session in a chiropractor's office in Scottsdale, not far from the Jin Shin Jyutsu school. I lay down on the treatment table surrounded by soft music and candles lit for relaxation and low light.

Elizabeth asked me, "Is there any place on your body you prefer I do not touch?"

I replied, "Elizabeth, I am so determined about releasing this condition from my body. I allow you to touch anywhere that's required, because I know and trust you will perform your healing work with respect and earnest for my highest and greatest good."

I took a deep breath and closed my eyes. While Elizabeth placed her hands behind my shoulders and knees—places where she was trained and guided—I began to see bugs leaving my body. She said these bugs were representations of issues.

"Just breathe deeply and allow whatever needs to happen," she said.

When the session was over, she instructed me to drink a large amount of water for the next several days. That same evening, at 8:00 p.m., I experienced pain in my right index finger joint and in my abdomen, in the area of my spleen. I held my hand on each area for a while, then fell asleep.

The next morning, Sunday, when I woke up at 6:00 a.m. and turned over from my side to my back, I heard and felt a loud bone-on-bone snapping sound at the base of my skull. It felt like my skull was placed back in the proper position, on its axis. I felt cold chills over my entire body. I got out of bed, ate my breakfast at about 8:30, and drank lots of water. By 9:00 a.m., I felt so achy I thought I had the flu. My eyes were burning, I felt tired, and my entire body was pulsating like a warning light on the roadside.

I called Elizabeth and told her about these symptoms, and she advised me to take a sea salt bath, as hot as I could stand it, for a minimum of twenty minutes, and to drink more water. After the bath, I returned to bed. Still in bed at two in the afternoon, in an altered state of consciousness, I saw my body turn into white light as it vibrated. The lower back pain worsened, and pain began in my upper back. An hour later, the symptoms resided in my lower back and moved into my left upper neck and trapezius muscle. I rested, ate fruits and cereal, and drank water for the remainder of the day.

By Monday morning I was still feeling worn out. During my 6:00 a.m. breakfast, I took an anti-inflammatory pill for the neck and shoulder pain so I could work at my computer at the insurance company. I called Elizabeth at 9:45 a.m. and told her about the pain and other symptoms. "Elizabeth, I've got to work and this pain is distracting me. What else can I do? " She told me to place my right hand on my left shoulder over the painful area and my left hand under my left hip.

She then said, "Ask what the pain is about, and soon you will feel a pulsation in your body. The issue is ready to leave your body since it is now up at your shoulder level."

I hung up the phone and placed my hands as Elizabeth instructed. I asked the question and heard it was about my fear and impatience about going up another level in my spirituality. I began to retch at my desk as the image of me appeared. The issue had to do with looking at myself, my motivation, control concerns, and the urticaria. The components of this issue were interwoven into this feeling of fear.

By ten fifteen, the neck pain had diminished significantly, and my body was chilling all over. At eleven, the pain was gone. I called Elizabeth back and told her the results. "Elizabeth, this works!"

I spent the next four weeks listening to my body in this manner. My cubicle at work was in a corner of the building where no one could see me process these issues. When these concerns came out of me, it lasted only a matter of seconds, so I could continue my office work without missing a beat. I also performed these sessions on myself in my bed in the late afternoon on weekends. I was guided by my angels where to place my hands on my body. Sometimes it was my knees, my arms, my neck, or other areas experiencing momentary pain.

As issues surfaced during these self-healing sessions at home and at work, I noticed there were traits or personality characteristics that revealed themselves to me. The first was the most difficult and profound issue to leave my body. I know it as anger.

While lying on my bed on a quiet Sunday afternoon, I closed my eyes, and through my third eye, I saw anger as a green monster in the shape of a male humanoid with bright-green skin and very long orange-red hair on his head, chin, and arms. The orange hair hung down from his arms about eight inches. The hair on his legs was half the length of his arms. His face was contorted into a vile, venomous snarl. He held a whip in his right hand as he held the reins of the white stallions of his chariot with the other.

I commanded, "Anger, leave me now and forever. I have no more use for you!" He looked at me with a scowl and left in a huff. I felt much lighter when he flew away.

The next three issues of impatience, irritation, and noncompassion were the most difficult to remove from my body. It was like releasing the cork in a sparkling wine bottle. It took several treatments to release them with bursting energy. Once this was done, the remaining issues flowed out of my body much more easily.

Impatience presented to me in my nursing career and work, projects, and communications with others. Irritation felt very much like impatience. Noncompassion was my misunderstanding about people who do harmful and negative behaviors toward me. At the time, I didn't understand people were and are reflecting myself back to me. Instead of returning the feelings of hate, anger, and irritation, I learned I must return the feelings of compassion, love, and forgiveness. I received counseling from my shaman, Lance, regarding compassion and messages we receive, interpret, and give to one another. I learned about change. Other people change only when I change. Their behavior changes because mine has, so I no longer need the negative behavior within myself. I learned more about how we are all helping one another on our journeys.

During Jin Shin Jyutsu treatments administered once a month at Elizabeth's office, my active role in this healing was to ask what issue I needed to acknowledge, learn, feel, and process. These issues prevented me from living an authentic, nurturing, and compassionate life. For me, this took courage. I first had to believe in reincarnation and the concept of past lives. Reading Brian Weiss's book *Many Masters, Many Lives*[5] helped me to accept the concept of life after death. I prefer to call it life after life because we never die.

I'm grateful for the person who placed this book in my hands and recommended I read it. This was something else I learned. People come into my life at the moment that is most beneficial to me. There are people who show up for a brief time and others for longer. Events occur at the moment it is in my best interest. This applies to everyone, not just me. I've learned that if I don't understand it at the time, I must wait, and the understanding will reveal itself sometime in the future. The key is to trust and wait.

Each time I returned to her office or spoke with her on the phone and shared with her the results of the healing and past-life regression work, Elizabeth began her response with "Cool, cool, cool!" Her smile and the enthusiasm conveyed in her voice confirmed I was heading in the right direction.

During one of the healing sessions with Elizabeth, I asked her, "How are we going to rid my body of this urticaria? What is the process?"

In an altered state of consciousness, she asked our angels and guides, and then replied, "It will be like peeling an onion. There are many layers."

I began to understand there are personality traits and experiences—both positive and negative—in our energy fields surrounding us that work their way out through the physical body in several ways. Bleeding, sweating, crying, disease, injuries, physical and mental conditions, and pain are several ways to process issues. It's difficult to explain this on a third-dimension level because space and time don't matter, and we are so much more than this physical body we inhabit. If Jesus is able to be in South Africa, helping a woman with a sick child in the hospital, and at

---

5   Brian Leslie Weiss, *Many Lives, Many Masters: The True Story of a Prominent Psychiatrist, His Young Patient, and the Past Life Therapy That Changed Both Their Lives* (Toronto: Simon & Schuster Canada, 1988).

the same time appear in the bedroom doorway of a woman in the middle of the night in her Phoenix home, after she saw the double doors magically opening all by themselves, then it's possible for us to be in more than one place—dimensions and planes of existence—at the same time.

For Jin Shin Jyutsu to work, what mattered to me was having courage to confront my self-examination. I had to be open to whatever information came through my altered state of consciousness. I told myself I had to face every dark aspect of my personality, no matter how repulsive. I was able to do this because of my intense motivation to endure even stepping into "hell" if needed. My goal was to be healed. I also understood no harm would come to me during the treatment, so I felt safe. I knew this process would make me stronger and make me a better, loving human being. It was necessary for my spiritual development. Deep down I am a good person, just like everyone else, no matter what.

I kept a journal and wrote down what was presented to me and where it was located or removed from my physical body, as well as the wisdom I gained during this healing. In past lives we had various personalities, just like there are many personalities in this physical world. Through reincarnation, we have the opportunity to advance spiritually in the human form by experiencing our lessons we signed on to in our contract with God. It's up to us which choices we make. I learned that, not only do we affect our life by our choices, we affect everyone on the planet because we are connected to one another. We even affect our environment, our Mother Earth. At this point, I'm giving only a smidgen of the explanation. What we do here in this dimension affects all of the other aspects of ourselves.

In addition to the treatment with Elizabeth, I attended a group spiritual communication session hosted by Summer Bacon[6] in Sedona, Arizona, the one who trance channels a spirit named James Martin Peebles, MD, NMD. Summer allowed Dr. Peebles to enter her body to answer questions from the audience. I asked him how I could rid my body of the physical urticaria.

He asked, "Do you feel pains in different areas of your body?"

I replied, "Yes."

"This irritation represents deep emotional reasons, and the salt crystals are remaining from suppressed tears. You set up barriers so you would never be hurt again." He gave me a ceremony to perform. Since he shared this with the audience, this meant others could also use the ceremony for their ailments, if so guided.

For the ceremony, I wrote down my fears in a question format and read them out loud three times. I placed the list of fears on a shelf for three days so my helping spirit guides could read them. I also asked my guides to read over my fears and to assist me in releasing them. On the fourth day, I poured water into a glass while asking my guides to imbue the answers to my questions about my fears into the water. When it came time to perform the last part of the ceremony, I asked my guides to place all the answers that were in the water into my body while I drank the water and burned the paper with the questions at the same time.

During this ceremony, part of me was very scared, very insecure, very tired, and very dependent on others to validate my existence. I needed to love myself. After drinking the water, the answers were clear in my mind, and I wrote them down. In the course of my life, I had allowed others to influence me to the point of not being my true and loving self. I wasn't standing on my own feet. I had much work to do to increase my confidence, courage, strength, and independence.

In one of the past-life regressions during a Jin Shin Jyutsu treatment session, I saw myself as a pathologist enjoying a horse ride with friends. One of my female friends jumped her horse over a stone wall, and it fell and broke its leg. I picked up a gun and shot the horse in the head to put it out of its pain. The owner of the injured horse arrived at the scene. When he realized I had shot his horse, he grabbed the gun and shot me in the right eye from a distance of about three feet. As the bullet fired from the gun came closer to my eye, I knew in an instant I would die. The bullet hit me with an explosion inside my brain, bursting skull fragments and brain tissue out the back of my head. During this video playing in my mind's eye, I felt the strong emotion of not being able to explain to the horse's owner that putting the horse out of its misery was humane and my intention. This frustrating emotion was my last at the end of my previous life. Through the healing session, I was able to let this emotion go.

Being a person with a controlling, super-organized, type-A, driven personality, I knew I had control issues. Working in critical care, I had to be in control, or people would die. Doctors depended on me knowing all the hemodynamic parameters, heart-rhythm interpretations, drug actions and interactions, disease signs and symptoms—and the list goes on. Always having to be in control manifested in anxiety during my air travel all over the world. The hardest time for me in the plane was the landing. I experienced sweaty palms, fear, and a racing heart until the plane was safely on the ground and taxied to the gate.

With Reiki, that whatever no longer serves us bubbles to the surface to be acknowledged and processed. When we increase our vibration, we seek to live authentically and with integrity. I was determined to meet this fear head-on and to do whatever it took to conquer it. I read a book by Guy Finley, *The Secret of Letting Go*,[7] and the concepts in it helped me learn how to let go of what I don't have control over. I had to learn how to give up control and surrender to God. I finally had to say screw it—whatever happens, happens. I also performed the exercises on releasing control. I had been such a control freak that my fear even blocked my progress to step up to the second-degree Reiki healing gift. My spiritual friends were encouraging me, but I hesitated. I wasn't sure I was ready—until Hoyt came home from a business trip to New York that turned out not to be for business.

Hoyt had been asked to fly to New York City for a meeting with a company who sought his services as a computer security consultant. When he arrived at the New York office, he was told he had missed the meeting, which had been held the day before. They apologized for not telling him about the change. Since the company paid for the trip and there was nothing to do, he took the opportunity to do something constructive and enjoyable: he visited the Phillips Collection at the Museum of Modern Art.

The driver who took him to the airport was a spiritual person from Haiti. As the cabbie spoke of spiritual matters, my husband said, "I wish my wife were here. You and she would get along about this stuff."

The driver looked in the rearview mirror and said, "I have a message for your wife. Tell her it's okay to go to the next level. She will enjoy it."

Hoyt gave me this message two weeks after he returned from New York. I was stunned. I knew this was a message from my guides, encouraging me to continue my growth and receive the second Reiki attunement. Our guides and angels work in mysterious ways, or so it seemed to me. Imagine someone flying all the way across the country just to retrieve a message from spirit. I wonder if our guides feel we need a profound method of message delivery to get us to act or to make sure we are conscious of it. I was also learning about divine timing—situations occurring at the exact moment for the best of all involved.

---

7   Guy Finley, The Secret of Letting Go (Woodbury, MN: Llewellyn Publications, 1990).

The confirming message from the New York cabbie gave me the incentive to take the Reiki II class. Ann gave me my attunement along with three other women in November of 2001. Through a meditation during the class, I discovered I no longer had to save lives working in a critical care unit or in an emergency room. I knew my life was no longer about death and trying to prevent it. It wasn't my job to stop someone from transitioning to the other side if it was in their soul plan. It was about living and helping people learn and process their life lessons.

During the Reiki II course, my female black cat, Shady Lady, became ill. She had allergy issues, and my vet told me to observe her and bring her into the office that coming Monday. I gave her Reiki energy and went to class the next morning.

When I arrived home from the first day of the Reiki class that night, I couldn't find her in the house. Hoyt assured me all the windows and doors had been shut and locked. He was adamant that she couldn't have gone outdoors. I went door to door in the neighborhood that night, showing people her picture and asking them to keep an eye out for her. No one had seen her. She was never seen again, at least in the physical sense.

When I returned to the Reiki class the next day, Ann could see my cat next to me in the form of golden light. She said, "Shady Lady is happy and healthy. It was time for her to cross over."

I asked, "How did she leave?"

"She just left."

I had to accept this, even though I didn't fully understand it at the time. I've since learned about translation.

Shady Lady translated on the Saturday afternoon while I was in class. Translating is the process of leaving this third-dimensional reality and going into the spirit world with the physical body. Jesus did this. Monks do this. There are portals, or gateways, into other dimensions all around us. I know of people who see animals and people walking in and out of portals in their homes and other buildings. I didn't discover the location of the portal in my husband's home until we were blessed with a litter of five kittens. The kittens showed me where it is, and I confirmed it with my crystal pendulum and from my Higher Self.

In Reiki II, we practiced sending healing energy to a friend who agreed to tell us later how they felt at a certain time when we students would be performing long-distance Reiki. I chose my friend Gabriella, because she is sensitive to this type of energy and we had gone through the Reiki I class together. She told me she'd felt the energy I sent across town that afternoon, saying, "It was definitely a soft, wavy feeling all over my body." I have since used Reiki II in healing both animals and people.

In February of 2002, a major breakthrough occurred in my Jin Shin Jystsu treatment. In this particular session, I experienced a memory of my dad beating me in my great-grandfather's barn when I was about eight years old. This beating with a leather belt was for my bad behavior at my grandparents' home. But I didn't know why I deserved the punishment. My angels told me my ability to be compassionate toward others left my body during the beating. When I acknowledged this memory and the energy attached to it, I felt drained.

Elizabeth gave me a homework assignment to recreate the movements of a child at play. I purchased a four-dollar plastic ball filled with air at a local toy store. Hoyt and I tossed the ball back and forth to each other in the backyard, running after it and picking it up and throwing the ball again. We did this for twenty minutes. Playing is healing, at any age. I've since learned that the experiences that happen to us help to release the karma from previous lives. In this life, I needed that beating to release the noncompassion from many lifetimes. So, the beating, for me, became a gift in this lifetime. I don't blame or judge my dad. What happened, happened. It is what it is and I'm grateful for the experience.

Just after that February session, I received guidance from my Higher Self that it was time to start decreasing the dosage of the antihistamines. When I discussed my disappointment in the recent increase in the price of the antihistamine with my pulmonologist, he suggested I stop the cetirizine and adjust the hydroxyzine to a lower dosage by ten milligrams. Over the next four months, I gradually decreased the hydroxyzine down to one ten-milligram pill at night.

One evening, when I experienced my whole body shaking for about twenty minutes while on the sofa, I called Elizabeth. She said, "This is occurring because you are releasing issues. You are shaking this old stuff out. You're going to be okay. Just breathe deeply and slowly, and let it shake out. You're doing great work here."

I felt much better just having her confirmation that all was normal in this healing process. If I had not been a nurse and a healer, this shaking episode would have been very scary to me. The closest description I can give of this shaking is that it is the same as the rigors of a high fever. I didn't have a fever, nor did I feel hot. And Elizabeth was right; I was fine after this episode of shaking.

My role in this healing process was to ask for the answers or meaning of the symptoms as they occurred. I had to learn, feel, and process the issues that prevented me from living an authentic, nurturing, and compassionate life. It was as simple as acknowledging that I am a different person in this life and in past lives. I had to remember that everyone on this planet is capable of change, even me, so I will most likely be a different person in a future life. In other words, I had to face every dark aspect of my personality, no matter how repulsive it was to me. I could no longer label what was presented to me as negative. It is what it is. Just that. No more, no less. And this required that I stop judging myself and other people.

When I felt additional pain on the left side of my neck, the personality traits of viciousness, bitchiness, and jealousy came out through retching. Arrogance came out of my back at the level of my first and second lumbar vertebrae. Pain between the third and fourth cervical vertebrae on the right side was a representation of being a liar and antagonistic. Judgment came out of my left shoulder.

From my mid-spine on the right side, insecurity, communication issues, being a braggart, being egotistical, and being lazy came out of me. Forgetting I'm a healer came out of my middle back on my right side and my left shoulder. Not being a charitable person came out the left side of my middle back, as well as feeling unworthiness in my creations. Judging myself as being stupid and controlling also came out of my left middle back.

Through coughing and deep breathing, I released the following issues while in deep meditation: lack of trust in other people, mischief, gossip, procrastination, disorganization, sloppiness, aloofness, being mad, sexual problems, stealing earrings at the age of ten, hatred, and impatience with the incompetence of other people and of myself.

From my lower body, I released a situation from when I was younger, when a girlfriend chose me to play with and not my other friend. The girlfriend not chosen was deeply hurt. While the three of us made a conscious choice to engage in this behavior, we were all affected. I felt remorse when I was told by the hurt friend's mother how her daughter felt. My relationship with her daughter became distant.

Fear of ants was released. My issues with my current husband, fear of exercise, being short and abrupt with people, authority issues, being picky, being a perfectionist, and prayer-and-meditation-resistance issues left my body.

My right hip released fear of dying, fear of the chest tube I had after the auto accident in 1986, irritation, and impatience.

Fear of tests was released from my right buttocks. Fear of forgetting came out my left knee. My left lower leg muscles released fear of not having enough money, fear of losing something, fear of having things taken away from me, and fear of lawsuits during my nursing career.

The left greater toe released my fear of my destiny and fear of the future in general. My pelvic area released issues that occurred many years ago. All these experiences and personality traits released at the exact moment and in the order I described, layer by layer.

The monthly Jin Shin Jyutsu treatments continued without a break until May of 2002, when I went to Europe for three weeks with Hoyt. While walking around the Zaanse Schans cultural village in Holland, next to the Zaan River canal, I began to experience nasal congestion and a runny nose. I felt more miserable with each step I took on the concrete path between the foot-tall grasses. I began sneezing so violently, and with copious mucous, I couldn't get my facial tissues out of my pocket fast enough.

I forced myself to appreciate this quaint tourist village because I knew I would if I had felt normal. There are green wooden houses and windmills from the seventeenth and eighteenth centuries in this village. People live and work in this residential museum. The sound of bicycle bells ringing as a family with children peddled by me on the path took me back to my childhood. I felt like a child again, exploring my world for the first time, like I had in Upstate New York. By the time we returned to the hotel room in Amsterdam, I was sick with an upper respiratory infection. I couldn't sleep or lie down in bed. I had so much sinus drainage I choked on the phlegm for most of the night. It felt as if I were drowning in water. I spent the next day lying in bed next to a large picture window, gazing at the billowy white cumulus clouds in the blue sky, feeling miserable. I told Hoyt to go out and have a good time and not waste the day. But he wouldn't leave my side.

I prayed and asked the angels to help me in healing, but I felt abandoned. In my mind, I asked in exasperation, *Where are you?* All of a sudden, I noticed the clouds through the picture window were in a formation of seven angels, each standing just behind the other, like paper dolls, each one smaller than the one before. I saw this as a sign. *They* are *here.* I'd just forgotten. And some healings take time.

On the 28 of May, when I returned to Elizabeth for a healing treatment in her office, I had been sick with nasal congestion for twelve days. As we began the session, I slowly went into a trance state, seeing a vision of myself drowning in the Zaan as a two-year-old child in a prior life. I felt the water enter my lungs and my throat close off. I saw and felt myself passing through a gray, swirling funnel. It was as if I were being sucked into the middle of a tornado, a tornado of death and surrender from this world.

In the next moment, I transitioned to my rebirth, coming out. Except this time, the funnel became a white Easter lily. I felt joy and the renewal of life. In that moment, my body was healed from the allergic response I had experienced in Amsterdam and the subsequent respiratory infection. My mucus drainage stopped instantly. My breathing was completely normal.

Elizabeth said, "Your nose is no longer the red color it was when you came into the office today." The rebirth was not only the removal of the illness and disease from my body; it was the rebirth of my spiritual development and consciousness. I was beginning to understand there are many levels and dimensions in these healing experiences too.

After this major healing was completed, Elizabeth and I continued for two more sessions, releasing twelve issues of distrust, disappointments, and pain from my first marriage. In the four years of mental and physical abuse from my first ex-husband, Jim, I had no respect, love, compassion, and forgiveness for myself. He was reflecting how I felt about me.

Six more issues came out. They appeared to be very close to the surface, as I used breath and retch to release them. My mother used to tell me a phrase in Polish when I wasn't sure what I wanted for lunch. It translated to "Go eat shit!" She repeated this to me from the time from when I was a little girl to my eighteenth birthday. She would never tell me what it meant in English, so I felt very frustrated and upset whenever she said it.

When I shared this with Elizabeth, she understood this to be very damaging to my body, spirit, mind, and emotions, because in essence, I was swallowing excrement or negativity whenever I could not make a decision. This programmed me to be negative to myself and keep myself in fear. When I released this, I felt much better and began to understand that this programming helped me to fulfill a karmic debt, and it helped me to be more compassionate and loving in my communication with people. This was the lesson my mother gave me so that I would become more compassionate toward myself.

I discovered I was very upset about my dad's arm being broken during his childbirth. His arm was never set properly and didn't grow to its normal length, but he was able to use this arm throughout his life with minimal impairment. I released this anger and frustration.

When I was eighteen years old, my friend Martha came to visit from Houston. Her visit was only one week, and I cherished every moment with her. My younger sister, Val, didn't have a close friend living nearby and wanted to hang out with us. I told her, "Go get your own friends!" I didn't realize at the time how hurtful this was for her. I would find out years later, through her husband, how this made her feel. I felt awful, ashamed, and saddened that I had behaved in that manner toward my dear, sweet sister. For a long time, I felt I could never do enough for her to make up for my insensitive behavior.

Now I realize just how strong a woman she is. She has her own lessons and intense experiences she still goes through. And yet she's still here. She serves elderly people in her career as a certified nursing assistant. She has the most loving, tender, and compassionate husband, who cares for her deeply. I realize her husband is a reflection of her. My sister taught me that one of the most grand and powerful traits to exhibit in life is compassion. This is her gift to all of us.

I received my last Jin Shin Jyutsu treatment on June 25, 2002. Near the end of the session, my head, body, legs, and right arm shook violently for a few moments. I took deep breaths, then released what was causing my left trapezius muscle to spasm. Elizabeth told me to surrender.

I concentrated as I let my body go limp. I began to say, "I feel, I feel, I feel…," but I couldn't say what I was feeling. I felt an energetic shift in my body, and I could see a multicrystal-shaped blue energy form trying to enter me on my front side. I said several times in my mind, *Go ahead, go ahead. It's okay*, as if coaxing a young puppy to jump up from the floor to the bed.

The blue energy form jumped into me. Elizabeth moved from my upper back and placed her hands behind my knees. I began to feel my upper body move in waves. I began to chant in a mumbling manner. The chanting turned into a strong Native American chant. I had no control over my vocal cords, and the presence was definitely masculine.

When Elizabeth moved her hands down to my ankles, my voice began singing as it increased in volume. This singing turned into a very feminine, angelic toning. The tone ended on a very high note. I took only one breath during this chanting, which went on for what seemed to be five minutes. I didn't have any control in what was occurring. I was told by my Higher Self that this entity was my Native American spirit guide, named AngelTreasure. During the toning, I felt the presence of angels inside me and around me.

Elizabeth walked from the end of the table to my right side and asked, "What was that?"

I shared with her what I had experienced. And then I announced, "We are done. I am cured of my physical urticaria." I sat up on the table, feeling very relaxed. My upper back muscle spasms were gone. This was the end of my treatment with Elizabeth.

I quit taking the hydroxyzine, and the next day, while driving to work on the freeway, I heard my Higher Self tell me to stop taking the birth control pills I had been taking for painful menstrual cramps, otherwise known as dysmenorrhea. I hadn't realized Jin Shin Jyutsu and the other healing modalities had healed all my physical ailments. I no longer needed to take any medicine.

A couple of days later, Elizabeth presented several case studies at a conference for psychologists, psychiatrists, and mental health workers that included alternative medicine techniques. After the conference, she shared with me that when she presented her case studies, jaws dropped. As of this writing, it has been ten years since I was cured of urticaria, dysmenorrhea, and seasonal allergies.

During the year of Jin Shin Jyutsu treatment with Elizabeth, I learned a couple of concepts that help reduce stress and build trust in myself and in other people. There were days when I was scheduled for a session and I knew what issue I was to work on. On other days, I didn't have a clue. If I were to choose which one to experience, it would be the latter. Why? Because not having a clue meant I had to trust whatever needed to be worked through, whatever was meant to be. The most profound healing occurred when I had no preconceived idea or desire of what I thought should happen. Eventually, I preferred not to know and just let what happened happen.

I also learned there are ways to work around obstacles. In one session, my eyeglasses were in the shop for repair, so I had to wear my contact lenses. I couldn't close my eyes in the healing session because the lenses would dry to my sclera. In this particular session, I kept my eyes open as I went into a trance state. The ceiling tiles disappeared, and I saw visions of people and places. I was able to keep my eyes open in a trance during the forty-five-minute session.

Healing occurs when there are two or more people involved in the process. While Elizabeth performed the Jin Shin Jyutsu hand positions, she was also channeling Reiki energies and much more. During each healing session with Elizabeth, I placed my hands on my abdomen and chest when guided. In each session, my hands felt as if they were deep inside my body, not just on my skin. At the time of this treatment, Elizabeth and I were channeling the healing energy beyond Reiki.

Since this healing, I have experienced head colds, muscle sprains and spasms, minor auto accidents, and so on. This is because we continue to experience and process our lessons through physical and mental ailments our entire life. What has made the difference is learning what the conditions represent and to be more compassionate, loving, and forgiving of myself and others—in other words, attaining self-love.

Chapter 6

DR. PEEBLES

Dr. James Martin Peebles was a spiritualist, medical doctor, naturo-pathic physician, author, and world traveler. He set up and ran heal-ing medical clinics in the United States. He was born in 1822 and died in 1922 at the age of 99.9 years. When he traveled and spoke about spiritual matters, he had a group of guides on the other side. He called them his "Band of Angels."

Summer came to the Center for Expanding Consciousness in Phoenix for a trance channel session in front of a live audience. At that time, her sessions were given in Sedona at someone's home. When Summer goes into a trance, Dr. Peebles shares his precepts of loving allowance for one another; honor, respect, increased communication with all life; and tak-ing responsibility for our life as a creative adventure. Then he asks if anyone has a question. Each person is allowed one question. Even though each person asks a personal question, the question and the answer are beneficial for all present. Additionally, the answers have many levels of understanding.

Ann received training from Summer to trance channel Dr. Peebles for groups. These channelings were popular among people seeking spiritual answers. Every session I attended was standing room only. In one of Ann's sessions, Elizabeth and I sat together in the third row. I concentrated on speaking my name in a clear and deliberate voice. Dr. Peebles acknowl-edged me amid the cacophony of people asking to be chosen.

I asked, "What happened to me during a healing meditation seminar performed by Elizabeth?"

"You got rid of more than you thought."

My second question concerned Hoyt's job situation.

"He will have to hit rock bottom before his situation is better."

After the channeling session, Elizabeth shared with me that she saw a beam of light come out of my mouth. It crossed the room and connected to Ann's mouth. I wasn't aware of the light beam, and no one else approached me about it.

Dr. Peebles gave me a meditation to open and expand my communication with my guides and angels. "Take the ball of light at the solar plexus and open your crown chakra [on the top of the head]. Let the ball of light go up through your chakras, up to above your head, then higher. Do this several times a day."

Another meditation I received in his answer was to spend a half hour in the morning each day and let the angels come in and perform healing attunements for my fears and any other ailments. I enjoyed the energy in the room that evening during the session. The love there was very warm. Dr. Peebles gave us a healing at the end of the session with everyone standing in a circle, holding hands.

I decided to have a private teleconference with Dr. Peebles through Summer. The following is an excerpt from the transcript of my first session with him on November 8, 2002. Dr. Peebles told me I was being asked to speak my truth. This was difficult for me because I was afraid I would lose family members, friends, and others around me. I had made a grand and glorious determination to walk this earth as a fully enlightened being. In order to do this, I had to speak my own truth to many people without fear. I have the ability to allow others to respond to me as they desire. It's important we humans all give acceptance and acknowledgment to life around us, and life will unfold as a beautiful and attractive experience. Dr. Peebles told me within a year I would be a changed person.

When I asked Dr. Peebles how we can be in more than one place at one time, he responded we can and we are. It's because we are not finite beings. We are infinite. This is the reality of our souls. We are here on the planet exploring the illusions of separation. We come to planet Earth and slow our frequencies down. Everything we touch, feel, and smell is us, and it begins to separate all around us. Then we learn to begin to love it all over again. And then we put this all back in our hearts. This is where we realize we find and touch the face of God. The rest is quantum physics.

What I was seeking in 2002 was simple truth. I graduated into a new conscious awareness that really everything is united through love. This is the frequency band I journey upon when I'm awakening others in the night.

From the time I was seven years old, I would sit by myself, close my eyes, and imagine nothing is here, not even the planets, the universe, angels, me, not even God, nothing. And then I would say to myself, there is no such thing as nothing. It gave me the heebie-jeebies. When I asked Dr. Peebles about this meditation, the split second before he spoke, the answer popped into my head. This space of pure potentiality I was pondering was love. There is really no such thing as nothing. The absence of light is not the darkness. It's the fertile soil. Dr. Peebles said it wasn't the absence of light, but where we plant our very being and grow. This awareness at age seven was enlightening.

From our conversation I found out I do this meditation to help others understand we can truly manifest anything our heart desires, right now. When we have this awareness, pure unabashed health will result from this. Our soul suddenly realizes there is nothing to be afraid of here upon the earth. We can have health for as long as we want in the human body, and when we make a decision to leave, it can occur in an instant, just like when we made the decision to come to the planet in an instant. This is what occurred with Jesus Christ. This process is called translation. We can learn to take our body with us.

My relationship with Mother Mary represents fulfillment, and all this is feminine. It is nature. The Blessed Virgin is very still and silent with her femininity. Dr. Peebles cautioned me not to fall into the traps of convention in our society of being a superwoman—trying to work myself to death. I have tried not to. Mother Mary reminds me constantly to be female. There is tremendous strength in the feminine form and the ability to be natural. He told me the Holy Spirit speaks very strongly through my body.

I was told my healing work was going to enter a different realm and that I would be incorporating my intuitive self in my work with people. I was developing very rapidly, and I realized I have an aversion to masters. There are no masters. We are all simply teachers, educators, et cetera.

None of us has to adhere to the consciousness of Christ or the words of Dr. Peebles. We don't have to embrace and embody every laugh that Buddha would exude. We can touch all of these aspects within ourselves and share them freely with the world. When we do this, we realize we are multidimensional beings and can communicate with the many rather than the few. We can listen to the music, the words of children that others would have an aversion to, and hear the ministry there.

Dr. Peebles shared with me I am working in this lifetime to embrace many perspectives, not just one form of healing art, but many forms. From this expansion, many people will come and ask for my services because they know I have the background. I've created a nurturing nest for others to step forward and be loved. Just like God. The embracing of many perspectives is the greatest healer of all, because it is there we are falling in love with all that we are. This is what I will be teaching.

I inquired about the trauma surgeon who saved my life in 1986, and he subsequently died of prostate cancer. He is working very hard to bring spiritual truth back to the earth. He wants to bridge science and religion, science and spirituality. He is a brilliant being and extremely technical in his knowledge. He did not fulfill his plans of creating machinery that can help adjust and alter frequencies in humans. He had a profound awareness and love of the field of biofeedback. He is still with me and says I'm a good teacher. I have the ability to speak up and speak truth. One of the greatest cancers upon the earth is when human beings hold themselves back and bottle themselves up. This is why cancer is created. It's extremely important for us to keep our feelings on the surface and all of our words and truth to flow. This keeps us healthy.

I asked Dr. Peebles if my angels had a message for me. He said the angels would never interrupt or interfere with my life in terms of spelling it all out or how it would be put together. Part of the joy and passion of life is that it is a playful dance. He shared with me that I get very frustrated with people, for instance while driving down the road. He recommended to keep telling myself at those points of frustration that everything is in right order. There is a reason why we can't breathe freely sometimes, and why the lines are not moving fast enough in the grocery store. When we realize there is power and purpose in every experience upon the earth, it's there that we surrender ourselves wholly, utterly, to God. In these moments we are no longer quick to panic or fear expectations. There is no distrust. All dissolves away. In any given moment, we can find power beyond our wildest dreams and imagination. We can go back to the space we call pure potential of the light within us. This is where we walk into the fire of our soul and find ourselves playing with the work we never dreamed possible. This is because we are no longer trying to make the world fit. There is great magic here and everything is in order. There is instant manifestation, love, beauty, and power beyond our wildest dreams.

In sharing my frustration of not being able to articulate my understanding of the causes of a person's pain perception, Dr. Peebles cautioned me to not have massive expectations of myself. I was working in a community that could not comprehend the concepts I know. The process of education for these people I worked with was going to take years. He said I found the language of the heart and I understand the sensitivities of the human soul. I understand the human body and the influences upon it. Other people have not been taught this. He said not to worry—I will find more humans who will embrace what I have discovered in my heart. Now I'm just trying to figure out how to share it with my mind. This meant I had to be courageous. No one else had been in the territory I was entering. He shared with me there will be times I will be tired because I will be called upon because I have the knowledge to give people skills so they can pass them on to others. He was referring to my gift of healing and guiding many people.

Chapter 7

OPENING MY GIFT

Elizabeth Kuester approached me about becoming a Reiki master. She offered to teach me the class and give me the master attunement. On March 7, 2003, I met her at her office, which she had prepared for the Reiki master class. I was the only student that day. She gave me a couple of handouts for the master to use in class initiations and taught me how to prepare a room for healing and Reiki classes. She gave me the attunement after I entered a meditative state.

After the attunement, Elizabeth wanted me to wait several weeks between the two classes she planned for my Reiki master initiation. I wrote my meditation in April, and I practiced the blessing techniques she taught me. This third level of Reiki felt much easier in the transition to a higher vibration than the previous two levels. Elizabeth decided we would complete the Reiki master course the following month. She wanted me to integrate the energies and prepare a meditation, incorporating colors, nature, and the chakras.

Life felt like a struggle for me. Maybe it's supposed to be a struggle. I still felt anger, fear, and jealousy, and I didn't know why. I needed to look inward. I meditated each day when I arrived home from work, sitting under the citrus trees in the backyard. In one particular healing meditation, I closed my eyes, breathed deeply, and entered into an altered state of consciousness. This is what happened:

I walk over to a tube of white light. The light is vertical, about three feet in diameter, and extends from the ground in front of me to the heavens above. I cannot see where the light ends above me. Standing inside the light, my body ascends like an elevator, up to heaven. Stepping off the light tube, I see gardens with people and animals playing and strolling on a path. There is a huge building formed out of clear crystal quartz, much like a Supreme Court building with grand steps. I am accompanied by my guide as I slowly walk up the steps to the entrance. I enter through the open doorway and walk through a grand hallway with a crystal ceiling, walls, and floors.

As I enter a room on the right side, I see all the Ascended Masters standing around a table, elevated on top of three steps, waiting for me. A physician suggests I lie down on the crystal table. I walk up the steps and lie down. Quan Yin holds my head. The trauma surgeon who saved my life in 1986 is at my side as the angels stand around me, performing healing. I see a large black mushroom cloud billowing up from my body, toward the ceiling. There are geometric shapes of energy in midair, which I know as healing symbols. The wind is blowing around me, so I let the debris from my body be carried by this wind, to be transmuted back into love.

When the healing session is over, I slowly sit up on the table, slide off, turn toward the Ascended Masters and those who assisted in the healing, and bow and thank them. They bow toward me. I walk out of the building, toward the light tube "elevator," and descend back to Earth.

I came out of the meditation knowing that my anger, fear, and jealousy were toward myself. I didn't trust myself because of what I had done lifetimes ago and what I had done in this lifetime. I had been carrying this in my energy bodies for a very long time. For me, it was difficult, and it took some time to release these toxic emotions.

Quan Yin told me, *"If this were all taken out at one time, it would be too much for you. You are in the perfect moment, now."*

As a benefit of this meditation, I learned that healings performed by light workers can occur in an instant, over several healing sessions, or even over years. The intention of the person seeking healing is one of the powerful ingredients in the alchemy of healing. The conscious desire to be healed is vital. And yet healing can and does occur unconsciously. All things are possible.

I learned how to perform shaman meditations. In these types of meditations, the person meditating enters an area such as a cave or doorway, and exits in a different area such as sitting on a beach or walking out of a jungle, for instance. In an early evening shamanic meditation, I sat in the citrus garden and lit a candle in a jewel-colored glass globe. The wind was blowing, and the birds were singing. The cats were snooping around in the yard. Holding a clear quartz crystal in my hand, I entered into an altered state. My guide, AngelTreasure, greeted me. For me, this meditation was most profound because I faced one of my greatest fears.

I talked with AngelTreasure for a while. He said that we must go on a journey now and we would be meeting one of my demons. To me, demons are representations of blocks or issues within us, not creatures like those in the movies or books. We discussed this for some time because I felt resistance inside of me. I finally agreed. I felt strong enough to do this.

In the next moment, we were standing at Shoshone Point, where Hoyt and I were married. I began to tremble and cry.

AngelTreasure asked, "Why are you crying?"

I replied, "I feel so much love and joy in my heart at this sacred ground, I am humbled with intense emotion. This geological area was sacred to the Shoshone tribe before the National Park Service took it over."

AngelTreasure told me I must trust him and I must hold on to him very tightly. That's when I knew we would be leaping over the edge of the Grand Canyon.

My whole body shook again, and I let out deep sighs of fear. At first I said, "Wait, wait, wait, wait…" When I had gained my composure, I said, "Okay."

With my arms around AngelTreasure's neck, we jumped off the edge. I screamed inside my mind, which turned into a realization that we would be okay when we landed on the ground. I surrendered to the fall and trusted him. We touched down on the soft, sandy ground next to Oak Creek in Sedona.

I recognized this area next to the suspension bridge in upper Oak Creek. It is the exact spot where I walked with a girlfriend when I was fourteen years old. We had heard a frightening growling howl from the woods. The sound didn't match anything we had heard before, like a bear or a wolf. We both looked at each other, then ran across the creek as fast as we could. We scaled the rock cliffs straight up to the highway. Our fear of whatever made that sound in the woods was greater than our fear of falling.

I began to shudder again, and I told AngelTreasure, "I'm very scared." With a nod, AngelTreasure motioned to me to start walking into the dark woods. As we entered them, I said, "I'm scared! I'm scared!" AngelTreasure reminded me I needed to meet this demon. So I was thinking we were going to meet the "demon" from back when I was fourteen. I really didn't want to see this creature.

I gained my composure and said to myself, *I am strong, I am strong, I am powerful.* I agreed to go farther. I held my crystal very tightly as we walked into the woods. I felt alone, but AngelTreasure said he was right there beside me.

I couldn't wait any longer, so I tensed my muscles and demanded of the demon, "Show yourself right now!" There was blackness all around me. Then a hazy image came forward. When I looked at the demon, I saw *myself*. AngelTreasure confirmed this. I stood there for a minute and realized I was fearing myself. "This is what I have been scared of? Me? How can this be? I'm love. Why would I be scared of love?"

I then asked, "Okay, show me what I really look like, outside of this human body." My muscles relaxed, and I started to see a flickering light. I saw myself as a wave of energy traveling faster than light and sound. My being looked just like a comet, traveling from left to right in deep black space. I also realized this star energy was pure love. I was and I am pure love. There is nothing to fear.

As a result of this meditation, I saw my true self for the first time: a star.

The citrus trees next to me spoke, *"You are releasing and being patient with yourself through this releasing."* At the time, I believed a lot of negative emotions would be removed from my body. I knew this was important before my gift-opening ceremony with Shaman Lance Heard.

* * *

I met Lance through Ann. He was an energy jewelry creator in Sedona who moved down to the Valley of the Sun. He is the most gentle and compassionate man I've ever met and a very powerful healer. When I'm in his presence or talking on the phone with him, I receive healing frequencies and vice versa.

Lance had told me he was offering his services to people to help them open their gifts for humanity through a shamanic initiation. I felt it was time for me to open my gift, so we set the date for my ceremony.

About a week before my appointment with Lance, my guides wanted to prepare me for the major transition I was about to go through. A group of bees delivered their message to me. I was in my office at home, typing on my computer, when a bee buzzed around my head. I moved my hand up in the air, redirecting a bee's flight path and leaned to the left quickly, dodging another's. Seeing four more bees flying around the room, I thought, *What the…?*

I looked over at my window and saw hundreds of bees crawling on it and on the wall. I looked down and saw about forty to fifty bees lying dead on the carpet. Of course, I was totally bewildered. I went outside and found a hole in the masonry outside the room, where the bees were coming inside. I put caulk in the outside hole, and the bees inside died.

I was very upset that the bees had been trapped in my room. I sensed this was more than just bees coming into my office. So I asked the bees, *"Why did you come in here and die?"*

I heard one bee answer, *"Dear One, it is our honor to come here to give you the message of a great change in your life."*

I replied, *"I understand. I'm still sad that it took such a great sacrifice on your part just to give me this message. When there are bees around me, change is coming in my life. All things considered, I truly love you and bestow upon you many blessings. My heart is filled with gratitude for your message."*

Later, when I told Ann about this bee phenomenon, she said, "Yes, bees mean change."

In the early morning of May 16, 2003, I entered into my shaman ceremony with Lance on a white quartz-filled mountain in Phoenix. The sky was clear blue, and the sun was warm. We hiked up to the top of the mountain, where a chair made of white quartz faced south. I received several healing attunements designed to open the gift I had brought to Earth, to assist me and people I heal and help in the ascension process we were all taking part in.

Each ceremony is unique and tailored by Lance's guides. Lance taught me healing procedures to assist myself and others. The ceremony was complete around three in the afternoon. Hiking back down to the parking lot, I noticed two jet trails crisscrossing in the sky. I interpreted this as a symbol of a crossroad in my life. I understood my life would be taking a new direction from the one I had been walking.

Before I left, Lance reminded me to "be kind to yourself. Be aware of things that will come up. You may feel like you're not doing things right, but just reaffirm and tell yourself everything is okay. Just ask your angels and guides about any concerns." He also told me, "You can ask your angels to give you attunements by lying on your bed and placing your hands over your third and fourth chakras [solar plexus and heart]."

When I returned home, I felt tired, but energized at the same time. I could feel a transformation occurring within me. There are no human words for what I was feeling inside and around my body. That evening, while I was still, my Higher Self told me, *"You're doing great, and good things will happen."*

On this same evening, a lunar eclipse occurred. While the moon was covered by the reflection of Mother Earth, I lit a silver candle in the citrus garden to keep the light reflected and said my prayers. This night was significant for me because this was the night I opened my gift of healing. I had felt pure joy all day long.

I woke up and looked at the clock: 2:47 a.m. I went to the bathroom and returned to bed, where I fell asleep briefly. Then, as I transitioned from the dream state to semi-awake, I saw myself lecturing to a group of human students in a seminar. I said,

Each of you is a facet of the diamond called the universe, called God. This diamond is very large and has as many facets as there are beings. Each is unique, yet each is part of the whole to create the beauty of the expression of God. Take your uniqueness and allow its expression in your shamanic healings. Let yourself be expressed in your meditations, your speech, and your interactions with one another. Another way to look at it is to see a large bouquet of different flowers. Each of you is a unique flower. Your petals, your color, and your fragrance are an expression of God. Together, you all make up the beautiful bouquet of God. This is what I see when I look at everyone in this room. You can see this too. See through your heart, not your eyes.

With my third eye open, I saw myself as a comet or star traveling through space, just as I had seen it in the previous meditation. While lying on my left side, I put my right arm straight out in front of me and followed the vector of the star until my arm was straight up in the air, perpendicular to my body. I began to draw symbols in the air with my right hand, with my arm moving as well. I did this for some time, and it felt as if someone else were moving my arm. This movement was done without muscles. My arm didn't lose feeling, even though it was elevated for some time, straight up. I lowered my arm, tucked my hand under the pillow, and returned to sleep.

In the morning, before getting up, I raised my right arm in the air. I began speaking a foreign language, a language not found on Earth. Before this initial experience, in one of my astral travels, I was on a spaceship learning a mathematical language used for healing. The language is spoken fast and it's a combination of sounds, clicks, and words I do not understand. The language is a form of sacred geometry, and it's running nonstop inside my body. I have the ability to push it back, so to speak, so it doesn't interfere with my daily activities and conversations. I can move it closer to my hearing range and to the point of allowing it to be expressed through my vocal cords in speech.

Lance and I reconnected on the phone after my gift-opening ceremony. My life felt like an emotional roller-coaster ride. I allowed myself to feel and release. Lance agreed I was opening up and releasing more issues to clear my body and energy fields. I was unfolding. He said my channeling would be better soon. The answers to my questions were coming easily. He told me the reason I didn't remember my dreams from the first two nights after the shaman ceremony was because I was taken very far away. My angels confirmed this with tingling sensations down the side of my body.

Lance suggested using "It just is" when I feel things and encounter heavy stuff—to just let it go. This is very powerful and healing. He told me I need to deep breathe as much as possible. He also reminded me I can place my hands on my heart and solar plexus chakras and lie down and tell my angels what is bothering me, letting them know if I'm tired, or nauseated, or whatever. They will listen and give me a healing.

He was right. I do this when I lie down to sleep. I experience downloads of energy shaking my body for about three to four seconds and causing no pain whatsoever. During each "attunement," my angels also tell me when they are almost done transmitting the healing energy into my body.

To assist in my spiritual transition, I engaged in several forms of healing. In June of 2003, I booked an appointment with an extraordinary Sedona healer named Susan Palmer. Susan is a professional healer, counselor, spirit communicator, and ordained minister. During 2003, she came down to Phoenix once a month and offered her healing services at a healing center.

On the day of my appointment, I developed abdominal pain around my solar plexus, and muscle aches. I didn't have much of an appetite, so I drank water. I couldn't eat vegetables or fruit. I felt tired, just as when I had a flu bug. I knew the Quan Yin toning session with Susan would help me.

When I arrived at the healing center, my abdominal pain was suddenly gone. I was guided to curl up in a fetal position on the massage table. I felt I was in my mother's womb. I heard my parents arguing. I turned onto my back and saw many colored lights. I don't remember any specific messages or visions, just the lights. At the end of the session, Susan told me I had gone through a rebirth. I felt much better. My energy was back too.

When I told Susan about the flu-like feeling I'd experienced earlier that day, she said it was a negative part of me that didn't want to be healed. It wanted to stay inside me. She said it was good that I honored myself by understanding that the healing would take care of the symptoms I experienced and the deeper issues I wanted to process. Some part of us attempts to sabotage our healing by creating symptoms prior to our appointment with a healer, causing us to cancel the session. People need to tap into their inner guidance in determining whether to receive a healing or postpone it.

During the next several months, Elizabeth shared with me that she had some hip pain. When she returned, I helped her move out of a bedroom in a large home she had rented from a wealthy family in Paradise Valley. She had run out of money and was worried she would end up on the street. I told her I wouldn't let that happen. I offered to have her stay in my guest bedroom with her own bathroom if she ever got to that point. I didn't want her worrying about having a place to sleep and food to eat. For me, it would be an honor to have Elizabeth in my home, and I told her so.

We took a couple of minutes during the move to examine her small rock-and-crystal collection. I picked up one of the rocks, which looked like an ordinary stone you would find on the ground. Nothing special. Elizabeth told me the story of this rock: One day when she was questioning the existence of God, she picked up this rock from the ground and accidently dropped it. It broke into two pieces. She picked up the pieces and placed them back together where they had separated. Magically, before her eyes, the rock became one piece again, with no cracks or lines of separation. She heard a voice say, *"And Elizabeth, this is God speaking."* In that moment, she understood and believed without a shadow of a doubt that God exists. The rock I held in my hand that day was her proof of God.

Elizabeth called me in the first week in June and asked me to give her a healing. On June 9, 2003, I drove over to the home she shared with a friend. I had just received my shamanic attunement, so I incorporated several shamanic healing techniques in a session for her.

When I sat down in the living room, I was shocked to see Elizabeth looking ancient. She looked about a hundred years old to me. Her remaining hair was hanging in silver strands down to her knees. I could see bald spots, and her hair was all over the room. Her legs, ankles, and feet were extremely swollen. We talked for a little while in the living room. She told me she couldn't have another X-ray because it burns a hole in her aura. I asked if she had any other diagnostic tests. She said she was receiving chiropractic adjustments only. The chiropractor wanted her to have an MRI, which she couldn't afford without health insurance. I was careful not to ask specific questions about her illness because I had been instructed not to. That morning, while brushing my hair, I had asked my guides about Elizabeth's illness and learned she was dying. I wasn't to say anything about cancer to her. Even if she brought it up, I wasn't to discuss it.

Elizabeth lay down on her futon while I washed my hands in the bathroom. The healing session I performed on her consisted of several modalities. Combining energy medicine, crystals, Reiki, and shamanic tools of the rattle and chanting, the session took just over an hour. When it was done, I sat quietly on the floor next to her.

Elizabeth shared with me she had been working with old programming and conditioning about guilt. One of her projects in this lifetime was to gain the ability to love herself more. She said she felt better helping people, but my guides told me to tell her she shouldn't be doing any healing for others at this time because it was sapping her energy. When we aren't feeling well, for whatever reason, we need to recuperate and regain our energy and well-being.

To this she replied, "But I need the money." I empathized with her. How does a light worker continue the work when the financial support isn't there?

She reported she felt better. I disagreed, but kept it to myself. I sensed and saw no improvement in her energy level. If she felt better, who was I to interfere with her reality, especially if it was a positive one?

I drove home and took a shower with sea salt to replenish my systems. During the night I noticed I had cords attached to me from Elizabeth. Certainly this was understandable because we were connected as Reiki master to student and through the bond that developed during the year-long treatment for my urticaria. She was in a very energy-depleting state and felt comforted in receiving energy from God through me.

My Higher Self told me, *"Your work with Elizabeth is done, and it is time to move on."* It was suggested I tell Elizabeth it was time to go into the light and return to love. This would allow her to return to the spirit world, rest, and review, then decide to return to a new, exciting life on Earth, in a new body, if she chose so. I went to the bathroom and had diarrhea. I was releasing Elizabeth. I cried and released more.

I felt I had to let her go, and at the same time I wanted her to stay. I knew I had to keep myself healthy and cut the cords Elizabeth attached to me. It is what it is, nothing negative or positive. I was okay with it. I placed green and violet light around myself. Elizabeth was still communicating with me. She wanted to help me understand about energy cords and how to handle them. She wanted me to take care of myself too. The cords flew off, returning to her with love and light. I placed compassion, forgiveness, and love into the area on my body where these cords had been attached. I felt lighter again.

That July, I received an e-mail from Ann several days after Elizabeth fell down and broke her femur in several places. When the doctors looked at the X-rays, they realized there was nothing more they could do for her. Her physician placed her in hospice on pain medication. Ann graciously notified me that Elizabeth was slipping into a coma and thought I might want to come and see her for the last time.

I drove to the hospice facility across town in east Mesa. When I walked into her room, I saw she was already in a coma. I heard her death rattle. There were other people in the room praying for her. I stood at the bed and held her hand. I told her I loved her. I couldn't articulate the enormous amount of gratitude in my heart and soul for the healing work she performed with me and the Reiki master attunement she gave me. I just felt it in my heart. Elizabeth crossed over to the other side later that week.

* * *

I attended an evening of meditation and music at a healing center in Phoenix, presented by Lance and another local shaman. The folding chairs were arranged in three or four rows. About twelve to fifteen people came to this event—more women than men. Lance began the meditation by giving an overview of his teaching and a specific message from Spirit. The two shamans played musical instruments consisting of a Native American wood flute, crystal healing bowls, and a didgeridoo, evoking a deep, relaxed meditative state. With the lights turned down, Lance and the other shaman led us in an exercise to further calm the muscles, nerves, tendons, and ligaments in our bodies.

I sat in the front row with my eyes closed. While Lance played the didgeridoo, he watched us. His attention was drawn to a blue light hovering over my head. He was guided to hold his hand in the air and wave his hand downward. Just as he did this, the blue light entered the top of my head. At that moment, a surge of energy traveled through my body, causing my arms and hands to be drawn up in the air in front of me, making symbols. I was in an altered state, so I don't know how long this took.

Later, Lance told me I was healing everyone in the room. Each person had some part of his or her body twitching. After this healing session, no one approached me or talked with me. Some expressed their gratitude to Lance and the other shaman, while others just left. I imagine everyone had their eyes closed, so they didn't see the blue light or my arms in the air. I drove home not understanding what had happened. I had no knowledge or memory of what occurred in the healing.

The next month, Lance invited me to come to the healing/meditation event again. By then, I had learned how to make the healing session last longer by securing myself in a safe position. I lay down on the floor with blankets and a small pillow for my head. This position allowed the energies to flow through my body, causing my arms and legs to shake rapidly. My whole body could be engaged in the transmission of the healing energies without me harming myself by falling out of a chair. I told Lance I would like to arrange the chairs into two groups, one on each side, with me lying on the floor in the middle. He agreed, and we positioned the chairs at a forty-five-degree angle so everyone would be facing the front of the room, where the shamans sat. I wore an amethyst crystal necklace to facilitate the removal of fear for everyone as the healing session progressed.

Lance shared with the participants that I would be channeling a healing for everyone. When the shamans began their music, I lay on the floor and progressed fairly quickly into a meditative state. When the energies began flowing through me, my arms rose up and formed symbolic movements. As the music continued and the level of the energy increased, my legs moved rapidly. I could feel the energies running through my body. I didn't experience any pain during this session.

I began speaking the mathematical language out loud. Silently, I asked my guides, *How am I healing people during this?* I was shown a movie of myself dressed in a long, white gown and holding a six-foot crystal staff vertically in my right hand. I led a group of people up a large, wide staircase made of granite into the darkness. I understood I was helping people to face their darkness, to walk through it and to be healed. I was not using the darkness for negative purposes. Rather, it is a tool or device used to communicate our struggles and challenges of this life and our past lives. Again, after this session, no one approached me.

The third and final session was held the following month. Lance called me with a conditional invitation. He said, "Barb, this time I don't want you to pay for the evening session. You are healing people. This is the purpose of the session. This is why we are gathered. Would you be willing to sit with us shamans?" I graciously accepted his invitation.

Lance opened the evening with a question-and-answer session. This time there were about twenty or more people. A woman spoke about her work exposing chemical trails in the skies and their effects on humans. She had a website devoted to sharing this frightening information.

Lance said, "To me, the chemical trails are just another form of love. We can decide to exist in a state of love, which is the greatest healer and protector from harm."

I already had this perspective before Lance answered her question. It just goes back to how we create our reality. If we live in fear, fear will find us in some form or another. If we live in light and love, we attract the same. And while the darkness is attracted to the light, the light worker is always protected.

One woman asked how I was healing people. "I don't know exactly how this works," I said. "I am channeling healing energies through my body for people. It's being done unconsciously on my part."

As people began to chatter among themselves, I overheard a woman in the front row tell the person sitting next to her, "She's really good."

The healing session was presented in the same format. I lay down at the front of the room on my blankets, channeling the healing for people.

It took a lot of courage for me to expose myself like that, to move around in a convulsive state in front of people, feeling like I was clucking around like a chicken. Yet I felt safe because I was among friends and people of like mind. I was still going through the learning phase of my form of healing people. There was much more to learn.

Chapter 8

SPIRITUAL TAI CHI

I didn't have one mentor sharing his or her wisdom with me in a structured program for spiritual growth. I chose several teachers to guide me on this self-discovery journey. I read metaphysical books. I talked with like-minded friends. I sought advice from my Higher Self through intuitive people. I gathered information from my guides and the Ascended Masters. I meditated on my reality and my feelings. I reflected on my everyday interactions with my family and others. All of these, combined with my intentions and positive perspective, promoted the process of the change within me, making me a more compassionate and loving human being.

One of the people who have helped me in loving myself and feeling compassion for others is Tai Chi Grandmaster Zaysan, whom I met in the summer of 2003. Ann wrote something in an e-mail to me about Tai Chi that piqued my interest in finding out more about it. I don't recall exactly what. Maybe it was something about how good she felt energetically after practicing this Chinese martial art for health, relaxation, and self-defense. At the time I joined the class, I didn't realize it would become a foundation of inner strength and peace for me.

On August 10, 2003, I attended a Tai Chi class for the first time. When I met Grandmaster Zaysan, he looked and acted just like anybody else. He wears his gray hair long in a braid, or sometimes in a long ponytail, hanging down his back. He has a skull and crossbones emblem in the middle of his forehead on the black do-rag hat he wears to protect his scalp from the blazing Arizona sun. He is both funny and centered. He also enjoys pushing buttons in his students to help them grow. He is simple, just like his mantra to us students: "Simple, it is simple." When I realize how complicated I had made my life, hearing "simple" pushed buttons inside of me, reminding me that buttons need to be pushed to promote change in my perspective.

On this day in class, I was at the temple with eight other students. The class met outdoors on a large lawn, and it was 116 degrees. The tall eucalyptus and elm trees mercifully provided us shade, but the heat still got to me. I almost passed out from what I thought was dehydration. I had worn long pants and brought just a small container of water, about sixteen ounces. Another student graciously refilled my container, and my energy replenished enough to continue the movements.

Grandmaster Zaysan showed me the first step in Form One. And that's all I did that first day—repeating the same step, over and over. When the class was over, we formed a circle in the yard. Standing silently, with our arms at our sides, we bent over and dangled our arms with our hands at our ankles. We dropped down to a squat, then stood up, while raising our arms without the power of our muscles. Our hands reached the sky above our heads, and then slowly we dropped them down to our sides again. We did this exercise, called *dan tien*, two more times. Then everyone walked back to the temple and sat down on lawn chairs.

Grandmaster Zaysan had created the temple with his bare hands and probably a shovel. He built it based on others in Mongolia. It's a modest one-room octagonal structure with a dirt floor, glassless windows, and a fireplace in the middle of the room. It's modest on purpose, so one is reminded we are all at the same level. We are all teachers, and we are all students in this human experience. Economic status doesn't matter here. The entrance to the temple has no door, so it's always open—like Grandmaster Zaysan's heart.

Several years later, Grandmaster Zaysan added a waterfall fountain and an outdoor misting system in the temple for the hot summers. The wood-burning fireplace was changed to propane. The lawn chairs became built-in wood benches. One student donated a metal dragon decoration for the backdrop of the altar. Another student donated a three-foot-high terracotta statue of Buddha that sits outside the temple under the tall chinaberry tree.

I sat in the temple, speechless. I couldn't think of a word to say that first day. I thought, *I've been a social butterfly with other people, yet nothing is coming out of my mouth.* I felt humble and insignificant, about the size of a speck of dirt. I don't know if it was the depth of gratitude swelling my throat or if I was too self-conscious to speak. Maybe both. I sat there on the lawn chair listening to other students talk with one another. Grandmaster Zaysan smoked his cigarette, talking, smiling, and laughing with the students. *There is much happiness here,* I thought. *They know something I don't. But I do know one thing: I have a lot to learn.*

Grandmaster Zaysan was born in Ohio. From the age of six, he trained in martial arts. At fourteen, he entered a monastery in China for twelve years of further training. After completing other adventures, he returned to America and opened a martial arts training school in California. Eventually he sought the warm sun of Phoenix, where he opened his martial arts school and named it the Temple of the Twin Dragons.

Grandmaster Zaysan was chosen and initiated into the Table of Ancients—a secret group of ten Mongolian monks whose mission is to uphold spiritual truth on the planet. He became the youngest member in its history. He was branded with the emblem of the dragons on his forearms after passing a life-or-death test. Grandmaster Zaysan's intense training and the death-defying test he took are described in detail in his autobiography, *Table of Ancients.*[8] He offers martial arts classes, counseling, Tai Chi and Qigong classes, workshops, survival skills, and one-on-one training, while he shares the ancient wisdom of traditional Shaolin Tai Chi.

I wasn't interested in the weaponry aspect of Tai Chi. I came for the meditation and physical exercise benefits. I didn't know I would be receiving much more than what I had expected. At first, I didn't know the Tai Chi taught by Grandmaster Zaysan is a spiritual-based form. From what I've heard, it's different from the classes taught in other martial arts schools. Grandmaster Zaysan's Tai Chi can't be practiced indoors either. Doing so causes one to absorb toxins from the walls, ceilings, furniture, and decorations, and from the other students. Common sense tells me this wouldn't be healthy.

I quickly saw that one receives a physical, emotional, and spiritual workout with Tai Chi, so I canceled my membership at a local women's gym. Once I learned the First Form, I saw that I could practice it any-

8   William Saldausky, Table of Ancients (Bloomingtion, Ind.: Tafford, 2006).

where I went. I practiced it in parks in California and Arizona, and even in South America. It's like having my own portable gym, and it doesn't cost anything to practice. The meditative movements enhance the environment through the heart-opening energy it creates. Why do our cats and dogs run over to us and hang out next to our feet while we're performing Tai Chi? They must love to soak up the energy.

The day after my first Tai Chi class, I returned to my cubicle at the insurance company. The air-conditioning system was broken that day, and many of my coworkers complained about the heat. But I had a new definition of hot: hot was the day before. I was able to work at my computer, and it actually felt cooler around my desk. I guess it's just a matter of perception. You think you can't endure a situation, a worse one comes along, and suddenly you're able to endure the first situation without much difficulty.

In the second week, the other students were talking about how firm their butt muscles were from the movements in Tai Chi. So were mine, but it wasn't from the movements. It was from the intense muscle spasm in my gluteus maximus. During the first week, I slept with ice packs at night to reduce muscle cramping and alleviate pain. My body eventually became accustomed to the new movements, and the cramping and pain gradually went away.

Two of the Tai Chi students recommended I receive an aqua energy treatment they offer to people. Conny, a healer from Europe, offers her clients an energy balancing technique. I had a feeling this was what I needed in order to feel better and to release blocks inside me. Yvonne, the other healer, holds a high vibration with a Chinese physician inside her. Even though Yvonne speaks English, the doctor speaks Chinese using her vocal cords. I agreed to experience this form of healing.

For the aqua energy treatment, we entered a pool with our bathing suits on. Yvonne placed essential healing oils in it. Each healer stood in the water next to me as they made a cradle with their arms and hands. I floated in the pool on my back with my ears below the water's surface. At first I felt a little nervous because they had said they may need to spin me in the water. They had instructed me to hold my nose if that happened.

I concentrated on breathing as Yvonne spoke in Chinese. They slowly spun me around in the water, chanting. With my eyes closed, I relaxed and concentrated on my breath. Conny kept telling me to breathe. I breathed even more deeply each time. My arms and legs began shaking. At times my whole body shook, including my head. I chanted, toned, and spoke in the mathematical language. My angels guided me to go with the flow of the healing. I saw my angels in the form of balls of lights dancing around us.

At one point I noticed three palm trees growing next to the pool, and I thought of us three women with feminine energy healing my body. I could see Yvonne and Conny extracting negative entities that were inside of me. At one point my neck was hurting so much I had to say something. Yvonne moved to my neck, and Conny my feet. Their healing removed the pain out of my neck. Later my heart was so full of pressure, I couldn't stand it anymore, so I told them about it, too. They focused on this pressure and told me a negative entity was wrapped around my heart. At the moment it released, I saw a circle of flames leave my body. After this extraction, I felt much better.

I don't know what Conny and Yvonne did with the amethyst and the Chinese writing stone used in the healing, but I was aware of some of the oils they placed on my body. The aromatherapy transported me to another level of tranquility. I was placed on a purple foam mattress with a towel on my legs to keep me warm.

At the end of the session, I rolled off the mattress and experienced my body feeling light and happy. I swam to the deep end and back. I drank more water, and we talked about the session. We all had smiles. Yvonne and Conny told me I was clean; there were no more entities in me. They saw a white light radiating from my body. Conny saw sparkles flying around me, and my eyes sparkled.

They warned me about not letting anyone tell me to let someone inside me. They told me about protecting myself with a polished sphere that allowed only love in and repelled negative energy. They also said I should hold positive thoughts at all times. Negative thoughts sent out would return sevenfold.

Yvonne told me that the negative entities made me ill the day before because they knew I was coming to aqua therapy to remove them, and they didn't want to leave. This was similar to what Susan had said about my experience before her healing session. Yvonne had called Archangel Michael to come during the session to take the entities to where they needed to be. She warned not to send entities into the light because they might not be from the light. Conny cautioned me to let myself twitch over the next several days and to breathe through it. She recommended not holding on to it, just let it go. I did twitch the next day at work and did the breathing. I did more at home. Yvonne estimated it would take seventy-two hours for the healing to be complete and that my heart chakra was already restructuring.

This water healing was perfect during the summertime. The combination of aromatherapy oils, healing stones, water, three female healers, and the synergy of our intention provided a powerful healing with gentleness, compassion, and love. Although I didn't have a technical understanding of the aqua energy treatment, I found I was more open to explore and experience my intuitive self.

Grandmaster Zaysan told me that as I progressed in Tai Chi and practiced it, I would lose friends, my job would change, and other changes in my life would occur. I told him it was already happening. Within the next three months, I quit my job at the insurance company after one of the vice presidents came to town and announced in a staff meeting that the corporate office had decided to phase out the nurse consultants' jobs to save money. He didn't know I was sitting in the audience.

After my third Tai Chi class, I lay down to sleep in my bed. Before I went to sleep, I closed my eyes and saw a picture in front of me. My third eye was wide open. The picture was a mixture of objects suspended on a television screen. I saw pots and pans and all sorts of everyday objects—even a television set from the 1950s. It also felt different in my head; I felt connected to this information. To me it meant creation. I would be creating a new way of living my life and seeing everything differently from what I'd known before.

Grandmaster Zaysan teaches his students Form One first. Form One is grounding and opens acupressure points. He assisted us in removing blockages and opening our energy channels wider. During one First Form class, through my third eye, I saw an opening with a narrow diameter. It looked like a hose, and I was standing at one end, looking into it. I meditated and practiced Tai Chi for the next week. When I returned to class, through my mind's eye I saw that the opening was much wider. I saw myself standing at the opening of a fourteen-foot-wide sewer pipe. How appropriate. I threw everything I no longer wanted into the pipe and allowed the energy and healing of what I wanted to occur to flow into me.

After Elizabeth transitioned into the Light of God, I wondered if I had to enroll in another class because I didn't know for sure if I had completed the Reiki master class. Elizabeth had given me the master attunement but not all of the teaching materials to conduct the classes. I looked in Reiki books in the local bookstores, hoping to find information about my situation. What happens if your Reiki master dies or leaves before the class is complete? I couldn't find a single author who addressed this situation, but I knew of someone who might help me. Angel Therapy Practitioner Jenny Cohen offered guidance for light workers wrestling with spiritual issues, not just your everyday angel reading. Jenny has the ability to see written information above a person's head when she is giving angel readings. She performed a demonstration of this gift at the World Angel Day conference she and Ann presented in October of 2002. I made an August appointment with her.

When I entered Jenny's fifth-floor apartment in Tempe, on August 23, 2003, she said, "Hello, you're an author."

I replied, "Okay," not knowing what she was talking about. I gave her questions to ask my angels and guides.

In reply to my first question of what I was to do about my Reiki master class notes, Jenny said she could see the Reiki master symbols above my head. "So, you do have the Reiki master attunement. As for the class notes, I'm not familiar with this area. I recommend you speak with a Reiki master."

I later sent an e-mail to a local traditional Reiki master about my predicament. She graciously gave me a copy of her class note instructions.

I spoke with my angels through Jenny about how confused I was about metaphysical information and procedures. I had read many books and attended workshops and received angel readings from various psychic mediums. I found conflicting advice about the same subjects. My angel's answer was so simple: "Ask for clarity and believe what *you* believe."

My Reiki master experience helped me further in understanding that not everyone requires a complete and structured course. So, it's up to each of us to decide what type of course best fits our learning style and to be open to changes and different methods of learning.

I began giving Reiki I classes in my home, starting with a woman who was four months pregnant. We both asked our guides if it was permissible for the mother to receive the Reiki I attunements with a growing fetus. We were concerned how it might affect the child. We were both guided by a loving energy—of the universal life force, in fact—that it would be beneficial to the child. After receiving the green light to go ahead, I conducted the class the following week. Six months later, this student gave birth to a beautiful girl, and eight years later, this baby is blossoming into a loving and caring child.

I practiced the Tai Chi First Form with extra movements for a full year. Grandmaster Zaysan didn't ask me to change my form. He didn't correct me. He just allowed me to express myself and perform the form with extra movements. He showed me how the First Form is done within the distance of the outstretched arms on each side. He even placed a PVC pipe on the ground next to me so I could see the distance in relation to my body. He was trying to show me I could discover my own form on my own.

One day I measured the distance between my outstretched arms and marked it on my backyard patio's concrete floor. I performed First Form and saw I was stepping out of the markings. So I decided to take one movement at a time and see how the form fit into the concrete markings. I suddenly realized I was adding more steps than what I had been taught. I had to discover this on my own. When I performed the First Form with the correct number of movements, I stayed within the markings.

In June of 2004, Hoyt walked into my home office, excited that he had recorded a movie for me. "I've been searching two years for this movie, waiting for it to come on TV."

The movie was called *The Gift*. (This is not the movie with Cate Blanchett and Keanu Reeves.) It's about a woman with psychic and healing abilities. She helps another woman who is being abused by her husband, and she performs healings for people.

After we finished watching the movie, I asked Hoyt what this movie meant to him. He said, "If you have a gift, then you are obligated to share it."

I took this as an open door to tell him about my gift. "Well, honey, I do have a gift. I have this ability of knowing things, of communicating with angels and such, and I have the ability to heal people. I will share this gift, all through my retirement and beyond." What amazed me was that Hoyt had looked for this metaphysical movie for me to watch. He was aware of my healing abilities before I told him.

At that point, I had been wrestling for a year with guilt about leaving Hoyt. After years of Hoyt's belittling me in front of other people, I knew in my heart I could not tolerate this any longer. I had been running both the old program of "he loves you and he's doing the best he knows" and the new program of "you must stand up for yourself; this is nothing personal; this is the grand act of love you both agreed to perform in loving yourselves." The old program brought tears, and the new program brought me strength and courage. The old program lowered my vibration, and the new program raised it. It was a choice. Should I choose the negative or the positive? When I understood the question, the answer became clear.

I sought the advice of a divorce attorney in Phoenix in June of 2004. I asked him about my position and what would be the easiest and most economical way to dissolve the marriage. He noticed my composure and compassion for Hoyt and myself, and told me that usually women came to his office in tears and feeling very emotional.

I felt I had to be strong. It wasn't that I was a calculating person looking out for my interest alone. I truly wanted to walk through this divorce with honor, integrity, and compassion for the both of us. The lawyer placed the box of tissues closer to me on his desk when he saw tears on my cheeks. These tears were not from feeling like a victim. They were from the overwhelming amount of love I felt for myself and Hoyt.

I left his office with the names of four divorce arbitrators. I spoke with each of the four to find out their fees and procedures, and I decided on a female attorney who specialized in preparing the documents herself, provided that each party had worked out the details beforehand. She recommended not using additional attorneys for each side because this would increase the costs of the process and delay the inevitable.

The next Sunday, Grandmaster Zaysan asked me, "What happened? What did you do? Your aura is different."

I told him, "I spoke with a divorce attorney." And I wondered, *How can just talking with someone change my aura?* It must have been because this was a significant step I had taken to change my life. Our emotions are not separate from our actions.

Finally, in July of 2004, I sat down with Hoyt on the sofa and announced my intention of divorce. "Hoyt, I need and want to end this marriage. I love you, but I can't stay married to you." Saying these words was the hardest thing I had to do in this marriage. Why? Because I knew he loved me, yet I didn't understand his behavior of belittling me. This was his way of getting me to leave. I also knew someday I would have a greater understanding of our marriage and our divorce.

Hoyt responded, "I knew a year ago, when you began Tai Chi, you would leave me. I don't want to get a divorce, but I will not stop you, if this is what you want."

If this isn't a gift of love a person can give another, then I don't know what is. We are here because we want to be here. I felt torn between loving Hoyt and staying in the marriage and leaving so that I could continue to grow spiritually. For me, this was an act of self-love. More than anything, I wanted this divorce to be based in mutual respect, honor, and love for one another.

Although I felt he and I were compatible on the physical level, we weren't on the spiritual level. I had changed. When one person in a relationship changes spiritually, the other is no longer in sync.

After leaving the insurance company in 2003 and being without work for nine months, I felt dependent on Hoyt's income, though he wasn't working either. The 9/11 terrorist bombing in New York had affected the research and development divisions of computer-based companies, which also affected Hoyt's work since businesspeople were hesitant to invest without a guarantee of future benefits. It was time for me to return to the workforce. Within a month of announcing I would be employed again, I was hired at the end of the interview for a medical claim review job offer in Scottsdale. The supervisor who hired me was also intuitive and knew instantly I was a healer.

* * *

Grandmaster Zaysan invited us students to go to the Feng Shui Festival at the Chinese Cultural Center (CCC) in Phoenix to perform a Tai Chi demonstration for the public. I told him I didn't feel I was good enough to demonstrate Tai Chi.

He said, "Most people don't even know if you are doing Tai Chi correctly or not."

I added, "And the masters who do will understand this is just where I'm at in my Tai Chi."

"Yes."

That gave me encouragement to participate with my fellow students, who had studied Tai Chi longer than I had. I felt having the other students with me would be supportive. It wasn't as though I would be performing before an audience all by myself. That would be frightening.

The morning I went to the CCC, I wore the long-sleeve Tai Chi jacket I had sewn, with black cotton and a middle section of gold tiger-print fabric. I found Grandmaster Zaysan sitting in a chair at a table, selling his books and promoting his Tai Chi classes. A fellow student Yvonne, was participating in the festival as a vendor, selling her aromatherapy essential oils. I didn't see any other students. I thought that maybe I was early and they would show up later.

I watched a group of people from another Tai Chi school perform on the concrete stage next to the parking lot. It was a cloudy day, with temperatures in the seventies. I was grateful the sun wasn't shining on my dark clothes. While we were sitting at the table, Grandmaster Zaysan told me to perform Form One right there, in front of him in the parking lot.

I asked, "Right here?"

And he nodded and said yes. My bladder was full, so I told him I first had to go to the bathroom.

I walked over to a store that had a public restroom. When I sat down on the toilet seat, I put my head in my hands and asked, *What am I doing?* I was scared to death to perform all by myself. *Why did I come? Why didn't the other students come? More importantly, where's all my confidence?*

Then someone inside of me said, with all the determination of a football coach directing his player, *"Look, you're the only student who showed up. Now get your butt out there and do your Form One!"* I complied.

I walked within ten feet of Grandmaster Zaysan's table and stood still with my arms at my sides. I took a deep breath and raised my left foot. I could hardly breathe. My body was shaking. Even my fingers were quivering with the nervous energy going through me. With eyes half closed, I could see people stopping their shopping and turning their heads and watching me. My nervousness was amplified tenfold. I reminded myself, *This is my form; this is where I'm at. Take it or leave it.* When I ended my form, Grandmaster Zaysan was pleased I hadn't fallen down. Me too. I felt shell-shocked.

At first, I wondered why Grandmaster Zaysan had me perform in the parking lot. Now I see it was a doorway I had to walk through. It did help me see that I can perform Tai Chi anywhere—on a rocky mountaintop, on a grassy hill, in parking lots around the world, in my backyard, in the desert, next to a river, and other places, as long as it's outdoors.

Chapter 9

HEALING MY FRIEND

In early September of 2003, I was guided to walk into a furniture and home decor store, where a woman from Holland, named Justine, sat at the register, reading a paperback book. She had dark-brown hair and high cheekbones. I stood there and gazed at a wind chime with green plastic dolphins. There were no other customers.

Justine looked up from her book and said, "Wild, isn't it? Have you ever seen green dolphins?"

"No, can't say I have."

"With the green dolphins and the sound, you get double the healing."

I nodded in agreement. I was intrigued with her awareness of the spiritual significance of the healing color and the sound of the chime. I felt I'd found a kindred spirit in metaphysical subjects. In our discussion, she gave me a precious gift regarding human communications: "We all play roles for each other in order for us to learn our lessons. Your husband's behavior is helping you to stand up for yourself and what you believe in."

At first this was a difficult concept for me to understand. It required that I look more deeply into my experiences with people and see beyond their behavior. I had to remember that we all truly love one another, even though we get into dramas such as anger, frustration, and hate. When people yell at me, they "sacrifice" their true nature as a loving person so that I will look deeper and listen to the message for me.

But it goes even deeper than this. Everyone is a reflection of us. When someone is mad at me and is showing me their anger, it's because I have anger within myself about something—whether it's not speaking my truth to someone or being frustrated with myself for not acting on a hunch or project. It's like someone pushes a button within me, so I become conscious of the issue, so I can work on it. At the same time, on some level, people can be angry because that is simply their state of being for that moment. It's possible that, on a higher level, they feel comfortable knowing that I'm a compassionate and forgiving person. They can act out their frustration and anger because I'm not going to take it personally.

Justine helped me to understand that another person's behavior helps us to stand firm in our truth and to love and respect ourselves. It's perfectly okay for us to walk out of a room when our loved one is screaming and yelling at us. We don't have to stay in that frequency. Ann relayed this message to me several years ago in an angel reading. I must look beyond the behavior and see the divine in the person who is screaming. The screaming is the sound of their pain, my pain.

On September 30, 2003, I woke up with my Higher Self saying, *It is time. It is time to do what you came here for.* My heart chakra expanded, and I cried with joy. I had just resigned from the insurance company. I decided to give angel readings, perform Reiki for clients, and teach Reiki classes. I ordered my business cards, feeling closer to creating and living my life purpose. And it felt wonderful.

I spent the following weekend in Sedona visiting with Justine and receiving a DNA transmission artwork she created for me. The encoded healing portrait shows the integration of the Higher Self and the Christ Consciousness within my being. The intersecting triangles in the design form a six-pointed star.

Justine offers this DNA-encoded healing art form to people. She receives permission from a person to access his or her Higher Self, and within a couple of days, a transmission of information is downloaded into her consciousness. She creates an image in color on art paper and mats it, ready to be framed. She told me one day she was guided to go to the store and purchase art brushes, acrylic paints, colored pens, paper, and mat. She has never taken an art class, yet she creates beautiful symbolic art from information she receives about a person. When any person stands in front of the art, healing occurs.

I decided to try my form of healing in public. I asked the owner of a New Age store to allow me to be a vendor at one of her upcoming spiritual fairs in October of 2003. This fair was a venue for healers and psychic people to come together and offer an introductory sample of their gifts to the public. I had been practicing using angel cards and my intuitive psychic skills and was eager to offer them to people.

At first, the owner of the store was reluctant to have me as a vendor. I wasn't sure if she had too many vendors already or was resistant to my form of service. I wondered why there was so much resistance on her part. I decided to accept her denial if that was what she wanted. I saw no point in trying to force this on anyone. Perhaps she needed more convincing or affirmation from her guides and angels. I understood her store would receive a portion of the nominal fee I charged. Then, just before the conversation ended, she agreed.

I arrived early and set up my card table and chairs with a lavender velvet cloth, away from other vendors because, at the time, I felt the mathematical language might be disturbing to other healers. At exactly 11:11 a.m., my watch fell off my wrist, onto the table, when a blonde woman arrived and set up her table next to mine. I took that as a message not to wear my watch, and slipped it into my purse.

This woman had large blue eyes that penetrated into my soul with love and understanding. Her name was Joyce, and tarot card readings were her specialty. She also channeled spirits. She had the most delightful and bright personality, with a golden heart. She placed a red velvet cloth on her table and told me her birthday was November 11. This synchronicity tickled me, as did Joyce's vibrant and positive energy. We spent the greater part of the day talking and swapping spiritual stories. Her husband, Derek, visited—another warm, caring healer with a tenderness that welcomes people to sit down and talk about their troubles.

I walked around and met other healers and vendors of objects used in healing, such as crystals and feathers. One was a red-haired woman who channeled St. Germaine. Later in the day, she came over to my table and asked for a healing on her right arm, where there was pain near the elbow. She had felt guided to come to me for a healing.

After the five-minute session, she said, "Just before you began speaking your language, I felt energy going into my arm. The pain is gone." For other people, I used angel cards and shared channeled information regarding their current struggles.

Joyce and Derek invited me to their meditation group across town. They shared their home with small groups of like-minded friends to experience various forms of healing. In the first session at their home, I lay on the floor while the language flowed rapidly from my throat. Some people felt their bones move, relieving pain. Others had visions of their home planet. Others wept. One woman saw and felt nothing. She didn't believe in this form of healing, and that was okay.

We also had meditations conducted by others. Joyce channeled messages from an earth divinity called Ashima. Ashima told us about the earth changing and how we humans are going to be affected in positive ways. She told us that nuclear bombs and weapons will no longer work because the physics are changing. I still get chills of confirmation in my body when I speak about this.

In November of 2003, I participated in a workshop by Susan Palmer for light workers who want to channel in their healing work. Channeling is a process of receiving information or messages from the spirit realm. She also gave us several questions, and we sent the answers to her by e-mail.

Including me, there were six women who came to this workshop. Susan gave each of us the opportunity to overcome our resistance to channel in public by having us practice channeling in front of the group. I felt very uncomfortable, yet I also felt I was in the company of supportive, like-minded women. Susan had "energized" the chair we sat in for channeling. When it was my turn, I sat down in the "hot" seat. Even the seat and surrounding air was very warm and loving.

I took deep breaths, closed my eyes, opened my crown chakra, and invited Mother Mary to enter my body. I felt resistance on my part, then an energy entered my body, and then I began speaking. I don't remember what was said. After the channeling, Susan told me before I channeled, she saw a blue light above me start to descend into my head, but it stopped. She wondered if I was going to allow it to enter my body. Then the blue light lowered into my crown chakra, and I began speaking. While I channeled, I felt an immense amount of love and peace within myself and in the room, including from the other women.

By the early summer of 2004, I had been receiving attunements for almost a year. During the ten months I didn't have a corporate job, I was afforded the comfort of privacy while attunements came into my body at home. Just a few moments before the energy came through, I would be given a message, something like "We have an attunement for you,

Dear One." If someone saw me receive an energetic attunement, it would appear to them as if I were in a seizure. My whole body shakes back and forth. If I had to, I could talk during these episodes, and I didn't urinate on myself. Trained as a critical care nurse, I knew these energy surges weren't seizures. I don't know how many attunements I received, because I didn't keep track of the number.

In the tenth month of receiving attunements from my guides, Ashima announced to the meditation group that I would be receiving energetic attunements with increased voltage. She said that when I completed the remaining series of "high-voltage" attunements, I would be able to stand up or sit while I performed healing services for people, individually or in groups. My guides had heard my request not to have to lie down on the floor for group healings.

In 2005, I had a lucid dream in which I was asked to heal a friend with a lower back injury. I began channeling the healing while speaking the mathematical language. Then my whole body shook as I stood in front of a mirror. I saw myself shake off the illusion of my human body and was left staring at the face of an alien being in the mirror: my face. In this moment, I realized who I am: an alien star being. I felt comfortable with this knowledge—a little surprised, but comfortable.

One woman came to my apartment and began to feel heart pain. Before she lay on the table, I channeled a healing for her heart. I became so hot I had to take off my sweater and wear only my tank top. Her pain completely dissipated within minutes. At the end of that healing session, she felt completely balanced and content, and said to me, "This was the most powerful and gentle healing session I've ever received."

Another client came to me for a healing. Near the end of the session, while I sat in a chair about five feet from the Reiki table, this client could feel me touching her gently while I watched gray smoke rise from her body. Her entire body was surrounded by purple light.

I've also been told by clients that their vertebral bones moved into alignment and their pain disappeared.

In 2007, I went to lunch by myself to a popular restaurant specializing in home-style meals. My waiter was a very kind and generous soul. He shared with me that his sister and brother-in-law were in jail for a one-year sentence because of their involvement with drugs. He had made room in his tiny apartment for his two nieces, ages eight and thirteen. He said he felt it was important to provide a structured and safe haven for the girls by establishing an environment of shared household chores, homework time, playtime, and prayer. He did the best he could on his salary, now being stretched with two more people to feed.

This waiter and I spoke about spirituality and the healing I give. His mother, who lives in Hawaii, works with crystals in healing people, so he understood what I told him about my healing gift. He said he was working at the restaurant until his lower back injury healed. He was making plans to move to Hawaii, where a job installing carpet was waiting for him.

When he brought my meal to the table, I asked him if he'd like a healing for his lower back pain.

He said, "Oh yes!"

"Then, just hold my hand for a moment." I closed my eyes and took a deep breath as the healing energy ran through my body. This healing took about twenty seconds. When my guide told me it was done, I said, "Thank you, God."

And the waiter said, "Amen."

I ate my meal and watched the waiter attend to his other customers. When three people sat down at the table next to my booth, he began to take their order. I watched his pen fly out of his hand and up into the air, then land on the floor at his feet. He bent over to pick up the pen without a wince of pain.

I asked my guide, *"Did the healing work?"* The reply was yes. I returned to this restaurant the following week, and the waiter told me his back pain was completely gone.

After receiving encouragement from friends, I decided to offer my healing services to the public. I created a website and fliers and had a brochure made and business cards printed. I traveled all over the Phoenix area and gave demonstrations to New Age store owners and healing businesses and schools. With the managers' permission, I placed my brochures and cards in bookstores.

Even with my enthusiasm and light personality, everywhere I went, I met resistance. This left me perplexed. I didn't understand why psychics and other healers couldn't sense my healing gift. Some refused to talk with me, while others greeted me with a harsh tone in their voices, as if I were wasting their time. I thought maybe I had set my expectations too high. Still, there must have been a reason for the resistance. Perhaps it wasn't my time yet.

I placed my ad in a New Age publication alongside ads from other healers. It generated a modest number of clients. But then I was awakened in the middle of the night by a man calling on my cell phone. He wanted to know how much I charged for my "services." The tone and vibration of his voice told me he was soliciting sexual services. I wasn't expecting this one, and I felt energetically violated. I immediately hung up. I found out later that this man had called several female healers in the same way. I pulled my ad from the newspaper and removed my website from the Internet.

There are all sorts of creepy crawlers out there testing us to be stronger. Since this experience, I've acquired skills and knowledge to prevent this type of behavior from affecting me.

I had a metaphysical experience on July 7, 2003, related to a vision seen in my meditation. During a massage with Nani, I told her about the comet/star vision I had after my shaman ceremony with Lance.

She looked at me for a moment and said, "When are you going to put it here?" moving her hand in the air above my body and bringing it straight down to the center of my chest. She massaged me, and when it was nearly over, she performed a cranial treatment. The treatment consisted of Nani placing her hands behind my head and neck.

Just after she did this, I closed my eyes and saw the image of the same star traveling through space, from left to right. Nani returned to the head of the massage table and placed one hand on the top of my head and the other behind my neck. The star's trajectory changed and moved at rocket speed toward my body. When it made contact with my heart chakra, an explosion occurred, and I began to shake violently and chant in a loud voice. Nani kept her hands glued to my head and neck because she was guided to by her angels. This episode lasted about thirty to forty-five seconds. My voice went from chanting to angelic tones.

Afterward Nani said she felt scared while my body shook but knew not to break the connection with her hands. I showed Nani the movements of my hands and arms in the air making symbols. I did not understand what the symbols meant. I just knew how to make them.

In March of 2004, my friend Justine and I prepared for a one-evening seminar of healing and teaching. We sent out fliers and made announcements at meditation groups, and I had several clients scheduled for healings the same week. I received a phone call at my mother's house from my friend Penny. She was crying and trying her best to keep it together as she asked me to come out to California immediately. In fact, she already had a ticket reserved in my name at the Southwest Airlines ticket counter.

Four days earlier she'd had surgery on her left foot for a bunion and a bunionette on the outer side of her foot, performed by an experienced and competent podiatrist. The same surgical procedure performed in Europe would have required her to stay in the hospital for observation of potential post-operative complications. In the United States, with our current insurance system protocols, patients must undergo the procedure as outpatients, thus gambling there would be no complications.

Penny was experiencing severe pain and swelling in her foot by the fourth post-operative day, to the point that narcotics didn't even touch her pain, even at maximum dosages. Her podiatrist carefully examined her foot, as did other podiatrists in the same office. They all recommended she return to the hospital for further observation and possibly exploratory surgery.

Penny has been blessed with a beautiful body; she's thin and five feet ten inches. She is very bright and married to a handsome, smart man named George, whom she met in college at Stanford University. After graduation, they married and settled in California to raise their beautiful and gifted children, a boy and a girl.

Over the phone, Penny told me, "You have a couple of hours to catch the plane. I need you out here to help me." I called my husband and asked him to meet me at the house to take me to the airport.

Two hours later, I was sitting on the plane, staring out the window, telling God, *"I don't understand why you are having me go out to California for my friend when I have healing and teaching work to do in Phoenix."* I wanted to be in two places at the same time. I received my answer immediately, when these words came out of my mouth: "I will understand when I return." And with this, I trusted that God knows what's best.

When I arrived at the airport that Thursday evening, George and their children met me at the gate. He drove me to the small hospital where outpatient surgeries are conducted Monday through Friday. I entered the room just as Penny was placed in bed and a morphine drip was inserted into her intravenous line for pain control. Her face relaxed when she saw me.

Her right foot was swollen and elevated on pillows. The skin on her swollen toes looked mottled, like marble. I reached into my purse and pulled out a bottle of holy water from Lourdes, France, which my mother had gotten on a European trip. I placed a drop of water on Penny's forehead and in the middle of her chest, over her heart. Then I began to pray and entered an altered state of consciousness as the healing energies flowed through my body.

The morphine began to work its magic in her nervous system and reduced her pain. I left her to sleep through the night, and then I returned to the hospital after breakfast. Penny wasn't allowed to eat or drink anything, since surgery was still being considered by her doctor. We took this time to talk about why this had happened to her.

I explained, "Sometimes things don't go as we planned. Even though your podiatrist performed the surgery perfectly and skillfully, complications occur. We have no control over these things. Things just happen. The best we can do is to walk through it gracefully. I'm here not only to help you heal, but also to make sure you stay positive, no matter what happens next. I already know you'll get through this and everything will turn out with the best outcome. You already know this because you asked me to come." I then channeled more healing energy for her.

The kitchen staff graciously prepared a lunch for me. While I was eating in the visitors' lounge, the podiatrist and his resident-in-training examined Penny. I was called into her room, where I agreed with the doctors that there was a bleeder inside her foot, causing the swelling and pain. Exploratory surgery was the logical step. I asked the surgeon and resident if I could give them each a blessing for the surgical procedure they were about to perform. They agreed.

While Penny was in the recovery room, the podiatrist and the resident sat down next to me in her room, where I had been quietly meditating. The podiatrist said, "I've never seen this before. There was no collection of blood in the foot. There was a clear gelatin-like substance. I just scooped it out and found no bleeders."

He then asked me about my presence there with Penny. I imagine he was wondering why she had asked me to come. I told him about my previous career as a surgical intensive care nurse. I also told him what I had said to Penny about post-operative complications and how a positive perspective is very important for favorable outcomes. I don't remember sharing with him about my healing skills. It was possible that he and I were communicating on another level.

He asked me to be in charge of Penny's pain management. He said he would agree to do whatever I recommended in regard to reducing her pain and promoting healing. He also shared with me that Penny was asking for the other foot to be operated on in the near future. He was amazed she was already planning for another surgery while she was still in the recovery room.

One afternoon, while I sat in a chair reading a magazine, Penny was startled awake. "I can feel you touching my body, but you're over there. I opened my eyes just after you touched me."

I told her this is just a normal part of the healing technique. My clients feel the same thing during healing sessions. I sit across the room, yet they can feel me and the angels touching their bodies.

One evening I went back to the apartment to grab a sandwich to eat and get my toothbrush because I planned to spend the night with Penny in the hospital. While I was eating my sandwich in the dining area, Penny called. She told me she was scared and thought she was going to die. I told her I was on my way back to the hospital. When I hung up the phone, I thought, *Why would she think she's going to die? It's her foot, for Pete's sake. She's not going to die.*

I returned to the hospital and asked Penny how she was feeling. She still felt scared and worried. Then I prepared the guest bed in her room so I wouldn't make noise after a healing session I planned for her. The nurses gave me an extra blanket and a pillow.

I sat on a chair at the head of the bed and placed my hands on her forehead. I guided her to relax by breathing in the love surrounding her and breathing out negative thoughts. I then placed my hands between her head and the pillow. Silently, I asked for all the dolphins of the universe, for Penny's highest and greatest good, to come for this healing. Through my third eye, I saw millions of dolphins swimming through the stars in outer space toward us. I asked for the angels and archangels, in my friend's highest and greatest good, to assist in this healing. And they came.

I went inside myself and asked, *What is my friend's fear all about?*

I heard, *"My dear, you are taking her into a past life and performing a healing. To her, this will feel like a death. Let her know all is okay, all is all right."*

I told Penny, "You are okay. I know this feels scary. Just take a deep breath and let it out. Let the fear float away." I felt the energies running through my body, and I breathed deeply, holding the light for her, holding compassion and forgiveness for her.

When the session was over, she fell asleep, and I crept onto the narrow guest bed, thanking God for allowing me to be a channel for my friend's healing. I thanked the dolphins and the angels for their assistance.

The next day, Penny's doctor ordered the morphine drip to be discontinued. She was placed on an oral narcotic for pain. Each time I went back to the apartment during those five days, the podiatrist visited Penny, so we kept missing each other. On the last day in the hospital, I spoke to the podiatrist on the phone. I requested an oral tranquilizer to help Penny with fear issues. I didn't know how to explain to him the fears and the resistance she was experiencing on a spiritual level, so I used my own example of the fear and flashbacks I experienced after my 1986 auto accident. Penny wasn't very familiar with my healing techniques, and there was a chance her mind/ego was scared too. I was grateful for the podiatrist's trust in me, and the tranquilizer did help to calm her.

When it became apparent to me that I wouldn't be returning to Phoenix for another week, I had to call Justine and tell her I wasn't able to participate in the evening healing session we had planned. I told her about the work I had been asked to do by God. I could feel her disappointment in me and the situation, and I felt torn apart inside. I understood I could be there in spirit, but I had to give this opportunity to another healer to substitute for my absence.

Upon discharge from the hospital, I drove Penny home and then went out again to pick up her medications at the local pharmacy. I created a medication administration form to document Penny's antibiotic, pain medication, and tranquilizer use. I also recorded her pain level so we could see her progress. I told her the goal was to wean her off the drugs as she progressed in her recovery. Penny's husband put two mattresses on the living-room floor for Penny and me.

Before her surgery, Penny bought a wheeled walker that looked like a scooter to me. This device allowed her to kneel with the affected leg, resting her foot, while she pushed off with the other foot. We met her podiatrist in his clinic every other day for wound observation and dressing changes. I enjoyed assisting him in the wound care. We watched her skin slough off and new skin appear. Her foot reminded me of a snake sloughing off its dead skin. The human body is amazing in its ability to heal and rejuvenate.

I used the term *Reiki* to answer Penny's questions about the healing I channeled for her. While I had the Reiki II attunement within me, I was channeling more than Reiki in these healing sessions. By the time I left California two weeks later, Penny was weaned off the narcotics and the sedative. She went on to a complete recovery.

The following year Penny underwent a bunionectomy on the other foot, rendered by the same compassionate and skillful podiatrist. I couldn't fly out to California for that second operation, but I used the skill of remote viewing during the surgery and saw the procedure progressing well from my desk. I was working as a medical claim review nurse at group health insurance company. When I looked in on the surgery, I was looking over the podiatrist's shoulder and saw the foot being operated on. I sent energy and thoughts of an easy and joyful surgery and of healing and a successful recovery phase for Penny.

On the plane trip back to Phoenix, it was clear why I was called out to California to perform healing work. I came home exhausted and developed a respiratory illness that lasted for a couple of weeks.

That following week, I attended a public session with Ann channeling Dr. Peebles. She learned how to channel Dr. Peebles under the direction of Summer Bacon. There were about a dozen of us light workers in the audience. I wrote my two questions on a file card so I could keep them brief.

I asked, "What occurred inside my friend's foot that caused the podiatrist performing the operation to find a collection of gelatinous material inside the foot and no bleeders?" I wasn't even halfway through stating the first question when Dr. Peebles started answering.

"You, my dear Barbara, performed a miracle. You do this unconsciously. You take people into their past lives, render a healing, and return them healed."

I was surprised the healing caused this phenomenon of the gel inside the foot. Then I asked, "Did my friend's podiatrist and I have a past life together?"

"Yes, you worked together on a project on the other side of this universe. This was a long time ago."

As a result of this healing experience with Penny, I learned more about who I am and how the combination of modalities such as the surgery, surgeons and nurses, holy water, prayer, Reiki, medications, intention, a positive mind-set, family working together in support and love, and the healing I channeled all worked to heal my friend.

A psychic skill known as remote viewing is related to clairvoyance. With the person's permission, I can remotely view surgeries. In other words, I "check in" on the operation to verify my angel's clairaudient message that all is well. When I couldn't be with Penny at her second foot surgery in California, with her permission I remotely viewed the operation for several seconds. I already knew her surgery would go well. I saw the surgeon performing the procedure and actually "felt" the sensation of the operation proceeding smoothly. Her surgery was a success, and she recovered in the normal fashion.

On a side note, before the surgery, I asked my angels if I had the permission of the surgeon to remotely view the procedure. I was told yes. If I had not received permission, I would have honored the surgeon and not peeked in. In addition, I already knew my friend's surgeon was competent and an expert in his field.

Chapter 10

PERU

On December 9, 2004, I flew to Lima, Peru, to meet with a spiritual tour group based in Michigan, called Sacred Trips. Hoyt graciously gave me the Christmas gift of a first-class ticket for my flight.

Before my plane left Phoenix, I asked my guides and angels, *"Will I be safe on this journey?"*

They replied, *"Yes, Dear One, you are safe. You also have two protective angels with you specifically for this trip. They will be with you on each flight you take."* The flight to Lima was smooth and uneventful, except for the dream-to-awake transition I experienced near the end of the flight.

In my dream, I was flying a spacecraft into an opening on the side of a mountain. This opening appeared to be about twenty feet tall and one hundred feet wide. As I approached the opening in the mountain, I very gradually woke up. I could still feel myself flying the aircraft, in the pilot seat, even as I became conscious. Usually a dream stops when I wake up, but this one kept going, even though I was partially awake.

It was one in the morning—rush hour at the Jorge Chávez International Airport. Eight flights arrived at the same time. I left the plane with the other passengers, and we boarded a bus that took us to the terminal. After I went through the passport check, my luggage arrived on the baggage carousel at around 2:00 a.m. I pressed a button at the luggage check area as instructed and received a green light to exit the area. Yeah! No bag check through customs.

As I entered the lobby area, men were yelling at the arrivals, hoping to snatch customers for their taxicab service. Then I saw Stacey holding a pink sign, Sacred Trips, and yelling my name. We hugged, and her good energy was welcoming. She introduced the man next to her as her boyfriend, Dana, a professional architectural photographer, and his energy was also very comforting.

We took a forty-minute taxi ride to our first hotel, Las Palmas, in a suburb called Miraflores, just south of Lima. After checking in, I walked up the stairs to my room, changed into my pajamas, and jumped into bed at 3:30 a.m. I felt so energized, I didn't want to close my eyes. My angels and guides helped me to relax into meditation, and then I drifted off to sleep.

I was the first tour participant to arrive in Peru. The hotel was near the marketplace and financial district of Lima. Restaurants with patio seating were just a short walk away. I woke up in the late morning and met Stacey and Dana in the hotel dining room for breakfast. I took two oxygen capsules, which were recommended to increase the oxygen level in my blood for our planned hikes at higher elevations. A breakfast of scrambled eggs, toast, orange juice, and tea was included in our room rate. The colorful Peruvian cloth runners on the tables served to wake me up.

Stacey, Dana, and I took a walk to a park overlooking the Pacific Ocean. El Parque del Amor is dedicated to lovers. A large terracotta statue of a man and woman embraced in a kiss stands in the center of it. The surrounding low walls have mosaic tiles with romantic quotes. On the walk back to the hotel, we stopped at the Marriott so Dana could take photos in the lobby for future business prospects. I saw a large picture of a soldier with angel wings, and I heard Archangel Michael's voice in my head: *"You are protected."*

I accepted the message. *"Okay, thank you, Mike."*

We walked to a restaurant and ate crepes for lunch; mine was spinach. This restaurant reminded me of the cafés in Europe. Eating outdoors next to Miraflores's central park was very relaxing, and the food was full of flavor and texture. After lunch we strolled through a book fair full of books—in Spanish, of course. Then we returned to the hotel, and I took a nap.

There was no air-conditioning in my room, so I had to leave the window open at night. That's when I noticed there was considerable noise in this city. I managed to go to sleep even though people were talking and disco music was playing in the bar downstairs.

The next day, Saturday, more arrivals came to our tour group. I met a single woman from Boston, named Glenda, and a married woman from Switzerland named Heidi. Stacey told us that originally the tour had eighteen people signed up, but through cancellations, it had become a "goddess trip" of six women. The bonus to our small group size was that we were able to fit in more sacred sites and activities.

Glenda, Heidi, and I ate breakfast in the hotel. Willaru, a shaman contracted for our spiritual journey, arrived from his hometown of Cusco and sat with us while we ate our breakfast. He is an Incan spiritual messenger. He told us he was born a Quechua Indian and learned to receive esoteric truth from his spiritual quests in the Amazon jungles. He is shorter than I am, his voice is soft, and his skin tone is a dark tan. I can feel love emanating from his energy fields. He was dressed in a long-sleeve sport shirt with a button-down collar and beige slacks. Willaru offers his shaman services to spiritual tour groups in Peru, and he speaks at conferences all over the world.

On our walk to the ocean, he gave me messages from the Masters: "Your separation and divorce is in order, and it is good you understand why and what will happen. Sexual expression is important, but it is necessary to be married. The sexual expression can be manifested through the breath. This is from the School of Mysteries. Anytime during this trip, ask me questions about your divorce. It is good that your husband allows your path to unfold, to allow you to journey to your heart."

I agreed and was glad that Hoyt allowed me to continue on my spiritual path. My mother once shared with me that, when she and my dad first married, she told him, "The door is always open. You are here because you want to be here." Hoyt and I felt the same way.

To us three women, Willaru said, "In nineteen eighty-nine, twenty-four Masters began coming to the planet. They are all over the world. They go around awakening people to consciousness."

Whenever we wanted to cross a street in this town, traffic stopped for us. People were so kind. I felt very safe, yet I knew that most traffic wouldn't stop for pedestrians. Still, it was best to be cautious and look both ways.

Two women from California arrived next, Alexis and Beatrice. Alexis was seventeen years old—a slender, sweet teenager with blonde hair. Beatrice was her aunt, a breast cancer survivor. A woman named Kathy from New Brunswick, Canada, arrived shortly afterward. She was a soft-spoken, older woman with blonde hair and the most wonderful sense of humor. I sensed she was street smart and wise about the world. We all went to a sushi bar near the ocean for dinner that night. I ate mouthwatering herb-crusted teriyaki salmon and veggies.

The next morning we boarded our chartered bus, which had soft, comfortable seats and a toilet in the back. Our driver drove the Grand Pacific Highway, a well-maintained paved road, heading south of Lima to Ica. Our six-hour drive through the desert took us through small villages where we saw the poorest of the poor.

There were objects in the desert for as far as you could see: three-sided lean-to shelters made of what looked like dried branches without leaves—or perhaps they were reeds—tied together with wire or twine. There were thousands of them about twenty feet apart, almost blending into the landscape if you weren't looking directly at them. Willaru told us people would come and stay in these makeshift shelters for a while and then leave, much like nomads.

We also saw businesses in small towns that looked like fortresses with guard posts. Political statements in Spanish decorated the sides of the buildings.

One image that remains in my mind from this highway excursion is an old, thin, dark-skinned man sitting on a lawn chair with his right elbow on his thigh and his head in his hand. He was staring, motionless, facing the ocean. As I looked at him, I thought, *This man has everything*. To me, he looked like Jesus Christ, if Jesus had lived beyond age thirty-three.

We stopped at a restaurant for lunch and had tortillas and bean dishes. This is where I began drinking orange soda with my meals. I drank so much orange soda during this trip Kathy said I had an orange glow around me.

When we arrived in Ica, the first stop we made was a visit to the Cabrera Ica stones museum. This small, modest building had a collection of over eleven thousand stones with carvings depicting spaceships, star beings, and dinosaurs. They were collected, studied, and protected by Dr. Javier Cabrera and his family. One carving was of a primitive elephant, extinct over a million years ago. According to David Hanson, who met

Dr. Cabrera in 2001 just before he died of cancer, laboratory analyses revealed these stones came from volcanic flows in the Mesozoic era (230 to 63 million years ago), and the patina of oxidation covering the engravings proved their antiquity.[9]

There were stones with carvings of scissors, scalpels, even medical procedures being performed, such as heart surgery. Other carvings depicted tall human beings interacting with dinosaurs. I asked Willaru about a group of stones with images looking like humans having sex, or at least having orgasms. I felt these drawings were for educational purposes or, at the very least, a way of telling us in the future that the information we know today is ancient.

As a nurse and teacher, I was fascinated by this collection. The energy in the rooms felt very intense and welcoming to me. Without the ability to stay and study these stones, I had to leave the determination of the authenticity of some of the stones to others more qualified than I.

We also toured the Regional Museum of Ica and saw skulls with elongated bone structure, as if they were "Coneheads" from *Saturday Night Live*, but not as pointy. Willaru explained how the Incas performed sacred alchemy to place the heart space into their mind area, causing an upward expansion of the skull. A binding cloth and rope could have been used to misshape the skulls too. We weren't allowed to take photos inside, and there were no postcards to purchase.

Our hotel in Ica was secluded in the sand dunes, with an oasis in the middle. There's a statue of a mermaid who lives in the oasis. Mermaids are in the same realm as angels and fairies. After we settled in our rooms, I went outdoors and walked up the sand dunes barefoot. There were people sliding down the dunes on pieces of cardboard. Others were hiking up the dunes for exercise and a great view of the horizon.

For me, walking in this deep sand felt as if I were walking through crystallized molasses. It beckoned me to slow down and just sink in. I sat on the dune by myself and listened to the mermaid: *"I'm still here. I don't perform my songs anymore. I am saddened because people quit believing in themselves. They have forgotten the love in their hearts is to be shared with all humanity. I will return someday, dear Barbara, and sing my songs of love and compassion."*

9   Ian O'Neill, "2011: No Planet," Universe Today, May 25, 2008, www.universetoday. com/14486/2012-no-planet-x/

She also gave me a healing. I could feel waves of loving and forgiving energy surround my body and pass through me. It was very soft. She sang to me, and then I sang her song, letting her voice become mine.

Before our group left our oasis hotel and headed for Nazca Airport the next morning, Willaru spoke about the circle of life in terms of the evolution of all life on Earth. "We are minerals, then plants, animals, humans, and spirits. The cycle repeats over and over. Humans used to be androgynous. Babies nursed from both mother and father because men had mammary organs too. The nipples are the remnants of their breasts. Soul mates were born together. Through evolution, the ego formed, and the last Incas caused the male to lose his breasts."

On Monday, day two of our trip, we were taken by bus to the small Nazca Airport. On the bus, we passed around a bottle of Dramamine to prevent flight sickness. I asked my guides and was told to take one. *"It will help, Dear One."*

Before we boarded, Kathy was very nervous. I told her, "I will place pink light around our plane, and my star being guides will protect us and our flight. We will be very safe, and we will have a smooth flight."

From one of three four-seater planes flying over the Nazca Lines—an elevated area of dry, windless desert with lines appearing on the ground—we saw figures in the landscape shaped like a spider, a monkey, a hummingbird, llamas, fish, and lizards. The sky was sunny and clear with some white clouds. Our ride had been enjoyable and smooth. When we landed, several people on the other two planes were nauseated because their rides had been bumpy. This all smoothed out in their bodies, and the nausea dissipated.

Willaru said more. "The ego limits us. The will of the Father is reborn every time we are liberated from the ego. You can create sacred alchemy by breathing while holding your nose on one side."

I asked Willaru to explain how the space vehicles land and take off on the Nazca Lines. He said, "Through the law of duality, opposite electromagnetic energy is used. There are stones underground in the lines that assist in this form of flight."

Our bus headed back to Ica, and we stopped at a sacred area in Nazca on the way. We walked up to a hill with rocks and looked over the ley lines. Some of the lines intersected the hill we were standing on. We took time and meditated there. Willaru channeled several messages for us from the Masters: "Stay on your path. Don't look back. Just like [Lot's wife], you'll turn to stone."

He also said, "A planet is coming toward Earth in 2019 that will change our weather dramatically. Not like an El Niño."

I wonder if this is the Planet X people are talking about. Also known as Nibiru, it was spotted by astronomers using infrared observatories in the early 1980s. They say it is coming into our galaxy in 2012.[10]

Willaru also said this: "Mother Earth gave birth to the Lemurians, who lived underground. The three fingers that Jesus holds up in his hand you see in paintings are the Father, Mother, Son."

Our driver stopped at the small Maria Reiche Museum on the side of the road. Maria was a German-born mathematician and archaeologist who moved to Cusco and began to study in 1940 under Paul Kosok, an American archaeologist who discovered the Nazca Lines. Her small, humble home in the Nazca area became the museum. She convinced the Peruvian Air Force to help her take pictures of the lines. She also convinced the government to restrict access to the area so it could be preserved. She died in 1998 after devoting over forty years in research and preservation of this historical, ancient site. Her 1960s Volkswagen bus is still there, right next to the house. I said a prayer for her and thanked her for her hard work and monumental achievement, not only for our benefit but also for the people of Nazca, who benefit from her legacy through tourism. I am grateful for having experienced this part of the world.

Willaru told me privately, "You are humble. That is why you allow people to say anything and you forgive quickly. This is good."

I asked him about the wars that keep erupting in the world turning inward—that is, instead of people fighting against one another over power, land, and money, the war is inside each of us. If we aren't prepared in our spiritual journey, great suffering will occur within us.

He agreed and added, "The poles will change. The equator will be at each end of the earth." If the equator is at each end of the earth, does this mean the land in between—all of the continents—will be very cold, as in an ice age? Time will tell."

Later we ate at a restaurant in Nazca. We also listened to a Peruvian group play music, and I purchased one of their CDs. That evening, when

---

10   Neil deGrasse Tyson, "The Cosmic Perspective," Hayden Planetarium, http://www.haydenplanetarium.org/tyson/read/2007/04/02/the-cosmic-perspective, previously published in Natural History Magazine, April 2007.

I lay down on my bed and Glenda was in hers, my third eye opened, and I felt I was flying over the Nazca Lines. It was as if I was watching a movie of space vehicles landing and taking off on the ley lines. I could see with great detail the color of the vehicles and markings, even a human-looking pilot with a helmet on, landing on a rectangular area. In that moment I understood why the shape was rectangular: to fit the shape of the vehicle.

I told Glenda, "Wow, I can see it all, and I'm still awake. I'm watching a movie of the spaceships flying in Nazca, and there are hundreds of them. It's nighttime, and the area is lit up with landing lights."

On Tuesday, day three of our trip, we drove to the Paracas area, where ancient people lived, preceding the Incas. We took a thirty-minute boat excursion out to Ballestas Island, a rock formation in the Pacific Ocean, where we saw diverse wildlife. We weren't allowed to land our boat, and we had to wear our bandannas as masks to cover our noses and mouths due to the abundant dander flying in the air. It looked like it was snowing feathers.

We saw sea lions lined up on the beach and draped over rocks, soaking in the warm rays of the sun. The rocks were covered with massive amounts of guano. If you can imagine many years of poop collecting from the wildlife nesting there, then you would see a mountain of white caca. There's actually a guano-gathering operation, part of a profitable fertilizer industry. Thousands of penguins, Peruvian boobies, Guanay cormorants, turkey vultures, and pelicans were sitting shoulder to shoulder, all squawking—everyone having something to say. Birds flying in, birds flying out. It felt as if we were at Chicago O'Hare at rush hour.

On the way to the island, we saw the giant rock formation called the Candelabra. To me, it resembled a saguaro cactus in Arizona instead of a candlestick holder. We were told it's more than six hundred feet high and visible from twelve miles out in the water. It is believed to be a symbol related to the ancient Paracas culture in 200 BC.

When we returned to the boat dock, we sat down at an outdoor restaurant overlooking the ocean for lunch. I had my usual orange soda and a sea bass-and-avocado salad flavored with lime juice. Willaru arranged for us to be entertained. A drummer sat on a wooden box and moved and danced as he sang a happy, energizing song. The breeze was slightly cool with a fine ocean mist. The ambiance of our light hearts felt wonderful. A young woman named Sonia came to our table selling jewelry she'd made from nuts and seeds. I bought a necklace with a human figure made of several types of colored nuts.

On the bus trip, Beatrice asked me to pray for her painful left knee. With her permission, I channeled a healing while I placed my hands on her knee and prayed. Afterward, she told me her knee pain was gone.

After we arrived back in Miraflores at the Hotel Las Palmas, I walked to one of the local money exchange businesses in town. The hotel desk attendant said I would get a better rate at an exchange office rather than a bank or hotel, and besides, it was after bank hours anyway. This was a good walk, and the exercise felt good after sitting on a bus for the better part of two days. Later I met Heidi and Kathy in the lobby for dinner at an outdoor restaurant just around the corner from our hotel. I had asparagus soup and garlic bread, and, of course, orange soda.

After breakfast on day four, we boarded our bus to the airport and flew to Cusco, the capital of the Andes. Stacey told us to walk very slowly off the plane and to the waiting bus when we landed. "The air is thin at an altitude of eleven thousand feet. It's important you conserve your oxygen consumption."

Every day we took olive-leaf extract to prevent diarrhea from the Peruvian water since our digestive systems were accustomed to water in the Northern Hemisphere. The water in the bathrooms had different organisms than what we were used to in our home countries. Even though we used bottled water to brush our teeth, the water from the showers had organisms that could penetrate our skin and our eyes, nose, and mouth. We were told the plumbing was old and not very well maintained. We were also instructed not to flush toilet paper in the toilet, even if we had a bowel movement. There was a trash can next to the toilet for disposal of paper products.

At the Hotel San Agustin International in Cusco, Stacey and Willaru checked us in while we sat in the lobby sipping a cup of maté, otherwise known as coca tea. This tea is made from coca leaves, which are used to make cocaine. I'm told it would take a lot of leaves to produce the same kind of high addicts receive from sniffing or injecting themselves with the drug. The tea is sometimes used to alleviate and prevent altitude sickness. Stacey suggested we drink one cup in the morning at breakfast, saying we would be able to hike without a problem. The oxygen capsules we took also helped.

Kathy and I roomed together at the hotel and for the rest of the trip. After we settled into our rooms, we took a one-hour nap. When I lay down, I could feel the tea working in my energy bodies and in my internal human systems. There was an alignment of some type occurring within all of me. It felt soft and comfortable, with no feeling of euphoria or giddiness. My third eye opened, and I saw many five-pointed stars. When I woke up, I felt clearheaded and rested.

Kathy and I met our group in the lobby. For a late lunch, we walked slowly through the streets and up to a restaurant named Granja Heidi. The owner, Karl Heinz-Horne, is a German man who came to Cusco and started a dairy farm. He opened this restaurant, which creates the most delicious and loving energetic vegetarian dishes. We drank another tea called maté, but there weren't coca leaves in it. Sweetened with honey, it was delicious.

On day five, we rode a small bus to the Sacsayhuamán fortress, which we pronounced as "Sexy Woman." We walked on huge stone staircases and found altars and carved stones depicting villages. Stacey and Willaru guided us to an area where we sat, and I felt the energy through my body. I chanted and toned there. Juan, our assistant guide, who has his own tours, took me to an area the Atlanteans had made. I touched the stones and felt confirming energy running through my body. I also saw alien inscriptions on the carved rocks.

We traveled by bus on the dirt roads the color of iron ore, and we stopped at an alpaca farm. I fed an alpaca eucalyptus leaves on branches and marveled at their gentle nature. This was my dream experience. I love the softness and cuteness of these animals. Hoyt had taken me to an alpaca competition north of Phoenix for my birthdays in 2003 and 2004, so I was familiar with these animals.

We boarded our bus again and went to the Pisac Market, where people sold textiles, purses, bags, ponchos, and jewelry. We met up with husband-and-wife shamans Lorenzo and Lucia. They guided us to the Temple of the Heart, high up in the mountains, where they performed a sacred ceremony for us. We ate coca leaves, and each of us blessed three coca leaves with our prayers. Lorenzo took our leaves and wrapped them up with the objects he used in the ceremony. He told us he would burn the bundle in a private area later that day.

We went to Tambomachay and spent time at the Temple of the Water. There we momentarily placed our fingers in the water flowing out the stone fountain and watched the flow change from a flat pour to a flow of water shooting up in the air as if it were coming out of a spout.

We changed the flow back to the previous direction just by rubbing our finger in the water on the fountain. I've never seen water behave in this manner.

We went back to the hotel and met Lorenzo and Lucia again. Lorenzo sold the shaman textiles he had used in previous ceremonies. I purchased a couple of them and small woven clothes. Lorenzo blessed the the shaman cloth. Lucia gave us each a good-bye hug. Her hug was so soft and loving, like a mother holding her newborn for the first time.

We stayed at a hotel called San Agustin Monasterio de la Recoleta in Urubamba. As the name implies, it had been a monastery. It was peaceful, with its central courtyard filled with plants and flowers. The grass yard, daisies, and hibiscus flowers gave us a beautiful environment for resting. Stacey had us pack a small bag for our three days at Machu Picchu.

At this point in the trip, I looked in my wallet, and fear came over me. I didn't think I had enough money to complete the trip and get back home. I relaxed for a minute and remembered I could talk to my angels. I heard their voice: *"Dear One, trust in the universe. This is your test."*

I said that I would trust. Every time this fear reared its head, I said, *"I trust in the universe."* It worked. I instantly felt relief from the fear each time I repeated the affirmation.

On day six we went to another sacred site called Salanniyoc. I walked up around the back side and sat on a large rock formation. I went into a trance and spoke the mathematical language out loud. A little Peruvian girl, who looked to be about four years old, approached me. She was speaking very softly, and I couldn't distinguish what she was saying. I heard her mother in the distance and imagined she said these words: *"Come back. Leave her alone; she's in meditation."* When I finished this transmission and regained my consciousness, I saw the mother lying on a blanket while her children played in the grass. She looked at me, and I felt grateful for her honoring my privacy and space by directing her daughter to let me be.

I gave her thirty-three nuevo sols—about eleven US dollars. From the smile on her face and the look of surprise, I sensed she was grateful. I heard a voice: *"And Dear One, this is how you are getting back to America."* I understood: as I gave this gift to the mother for giving me the gift of honor and respect, the universe gave me tenfold. My fear of lack on this trip was abolished.

We boarded our bus for Moray, the Temple of the Mother Earth. This temple reminded me of the circular copper mines in Arizona. The concentric terraces spiral down, deep into the earth, reflecting the journey into our hearts. The grass-covered terraces had carved stones arranged in a staircase formation, connecting each level. Grandmaster Zaysan had prepared me for my trip to Peru in a way I didn't understand until the memory of walking blindfolded on a two-by-four came to mind when I saw the flying stairs.

One night during Tai Chi class, Grandmaster Zaysan had instructed us students to walk forward and backward, blindfolded, on a two-by-four piece of wood elevated about eight inches above the ground on cement blocks. I had to trust my steps, and it wasn't easy. I felt the moral support of my fellow students and Grandmaster Zaysan keeping me from falling off. I don't remember whether I fell off the wood, but it doesn't matter. When I entered the Mother Earth Temple in Peru, I stepped down the flying stone stairs, which were set about a foot apart. I felt confident as I stepped easily and quickly without holding on to the wall.

At the bottom of the temple was a large, circular grass field. There we celebrated within ourselves and felt the connection to Mother Earth and the cosmos. We lay down on the grass and meditated. The sun was warm on my face, and the air was cool. We held hands and chanted three times. I was guided to move my arms up in the air in formations. My third eye opened, and I saw a golden sparkling star hovering over me. Then I saw myself ascending a staircase leading to a stone pyramid. I felt I had returned home. Willaru motioned us to walk up out of the temple and return to the bus. I didn't want to leave, but I knew there were more magical places to experience.

The Maras salt mines were an awesome sight. We hiked down to where salt water was pouring out of the mountain rocks. I anointed my forehead with the cool, salty water. When it dries on your skin, a white residue of salt is left. We saw about two hundred salt fields, all connected in a patchwork formation on the side of the hill, atop a valley between two mountains. We were told a co-op of village people mine the salt for their income. On the day of our visit, one woman with a baby strapped to her back was harvesting salt.

We left the salt mines and headed back to our hotel. We passed people walking burros alongside the road as we traveled in the Sacred Valley, which felt like the middle of nowhere. I had just said to myself, *Barb, you are finally living*, when our bus broke down. I hoped that we would ride burros back to our hotel, lugging our baggage. But we were told it was just a gas line that had come apart when it hit a rock. While our driver repaired the line, Willaru took the twenty minutes to talk about esoteric concepts that I cannot remember now. I didn't take any notes. I just listened and absorbed.

On day seven, we woke up at four in the morning. There was no hot water for a shower, so I took a sponge bath. We ate breakfast and boarded the bus to the train station. Our group sat on the train, waiting to go, until we were told our train wasn't running. We were transferred by automobile to the next town, Ollantaytambo. Willaru sat in the front passenger seat, while three of us women sat in the back. We did not stop to tour Ollantaytambo at this time.

I noticed the driver had a picture of Jesus taped over the speedometer. It was just as well; he drove very fast. Jesus said to me, *"You don't want to know."* I laughed.

I saw dogs, cattle, and an abundance of life, spirit, and soul in the village of red clay houses. The entire street was made of cobblestones, making the ride very bumpy. When our car passed a sign warning of speed bumps ahead, I asked myself, *Why? The whole road is a speed bump.* Just like life. Just like our path.

I had become nauseated, but it passed quickly when I boarded the train, sitting up front with Kathy. The front window gave us a great view of the landscape. The two-and-a-half-hour ride passed near an ancient ruin of a castle built on the side of the mountain, made entirely of rose quartz. I would have loved to hike up there and sit in one of the rooms. I imagine it must be a very sacred place.

We ate a boxed meal on the train and arrived in Aguas Calientes, our destination at the end of the train track. Aguas Calientes is the small village at the base of Machu Picchu. Kathy and I roomed together again at the El Presidente hotel. Our second-floor room had a balcony overlooking the sacred Urubamba River. There were about a hundred people living in this small town, accessible only by foot or train. An entire town without vehicles—imagine that. Sprinkles of rain came down while we enjoyed sharing a large pizza in the plaza.

Later we boarded buses that traveled the narrow gravel road up the mountain to Machu Picchu. We posed for a group photo and said a prayer at the prayer wall just inside the entrance. Willaru spoke of the time this place was a Mystery School where people learned how to astral travel and teleport to other dimensions. We walked around the ruins, then headed back to our hotel room for a relaxing soak in the natural hot springs.

Kathy and I found a small restaurant in town that served trout with avocados. That night we left our balcony door open so we could hear the surging roar of the rapids. Whether it's ocean waves crashing on the shore, gentle rain, or noisy rapids, the sound of water lulls me to sleep.

On day eight, the morning air felt as refreshing as a plunge into a cold swimming pool. From our balcony we could see faces in the woodland mist. I felt these images were mountain spirits. We took the bus back up to Machu Picchu, where Willaru took several of us into the Temple of the Heart, and we chanted *om* together. I left my body and flew through the rock and up to Wayna Picchu, the peak overlooking the ruins. The view from this vantage point was beautiful. The fog at that altitude gave me an ethereal feeling, as if I were in heaven. Toward the end of our chanting, I flew back into my body.

We hiked up and down the staircases. We practiced flying on a rock pedestal made for that purpose. The rock formation protrudes from the mountainside where there is a sheer drop-off of a thousand feet or more. Stacey and Willaru positioned themselves to assist everyone in taking turns in this risky experience.

We walked through the high, wet Amazon jungle. I wasn't aware there were two Amazon jungles, one high and the other down below, by the river. The path was muddy and narrow with dense trees and bushes all around. Across the valley we saw a narrow wooden bridge set against the rock wall of the mountain. A portion of the wood was gone. This, we were told, was a portion of the ancient Inca Trail.

At Machu Picchu, it's possible to look over to the neighboring mountain and see the image of an elephant, complete with a black eye formation in the rock. Llamas were brought up to Machu Picchu to graze on the grass; they are the physical inhabitants of this sacred place. They brought their heads high in the air when I took photos of them.

As a group, we walked over to a part of the city where a staircase is connected to the building structure, along the edge of the mountain. Kathy was very scared. I gave her a healing and removed the essence of the past life left over from a fall there. After that, she walked down the stairs without fear.

Juan took us to his favorite meditation area, where I spoke with the Inca gods and masters. They suggested an affirmation for me to repeat to myself during the week: "I trust the universe at all times." They spoke about my prior conditioning and beliefs regarding money, trust, and abundance. It was a matter of embracing a different perspective—a perspective of abundance and trust that all will be provided. It's so easy to slip back into old programs, especially when the people around us give judgment and have a belief system of guilt and worry.

We ate dinner at an Indian restaurant with French-style Peruvian food. I ordered garlic toast with a white sauce, cooked tomatoes over rice, and sliced baked potatoes with oregano and pepper. Afterward we walked to a shaman's healing room and participated in a ceremony that lasted about forty-five minutes. We sat on the floor, on multicolored cushions. The room was lit with just a candle and a light source shining colored prisms in the room. During the meditation ceremony, I heard singing bowls, drumming, Native American chanting, clicking sounds, and bells.

Through my third eye, I saw a black stick-figure medicine man. I chanted, *I am love*, repeatedly and left my physical body. While I was flying through the universe, out among the stars and deep space, the shaman showered us with flower water sprayed from his mouth. When we came out of the trance, I felt a poking sensation in my left buttocks. I reached down and pulled a sewing needle out of my skin, which I handed to the shaman. It had pierced through my pants. I had no pain or complications from this "injection." We left a love offering and blessed the shaman as we walked outdoors and strolled back to our hotel.

On Monday, day nine, we woke up at four in the morning. After breakfast at five, Stacey told me we would not perform the solstice ceremony at the top of Wayna Picchu since the fog was almost at ground level. We were given this day to do as we wished. I had coffee at a restaurant up the street. Heidi went with Kathy and me back up to Machu Picchu. This time, Kathy brought her clear and rose quartz crystals and placed them in the east window of the Temple of the Heart. We meditated.

While exploring this temple, I found a large hand impression in a stone bench and placed my hand in it. Information flowed into my mind. I immediately understood the handprint was from a male Lemurian who had built this temple. He told me his name was Amok. I began speaking the mathematical language and was told about our purpose: to teach and serve in love. We were told to come back to the temple in spirit and that it is in our heart space at all times. I began singing tones. We could feel Jesus Christ's sacred heart within us. I thanked Amok for the information he shared with me about the temple and the blessings we received there.

The next morning we met in the lobby to wait for the train. Willaru had fallen in the hot springs the night before and injured his left shin, which was bandaged. I performed a healing on his leg in the lobby, feeling the energies flowing through my body and into and out of my hands on his leg.

Before the trip, I had asked my doctor's office for an antibiotic prescription in case I got sick. The office nurse responded with a stern comment: "We do not give out antibiotic prescriptions indiscriminately."

At first I thought this was odd since my doctor had told me to ask for the prescription when I went on a trip to another country; in my previous travels, I had invariably come down with a respiratory infection. When I realized I wouldn't have an antibiotic if I became ill, I remembered I was traveling to a place in the world where medicines come from the Amazon jungle. I said to myself, *If I need medicine, there will be shamans to heal me.* In retrospect, I was the one who performed healings in Peru, and I didn't get sick. Perhaps the office nurse knew something I didn't.

We returned by train to our monastery hotel. I walked around the grounds and saw a couple of men making adobe bricks out of mud behind the building. I talked with a llama tethered to a rope behind the monastery. This llama gave me healing, and I reciprocated.

We spent time resting and meditating. Each room had a wooden chair just outside the door, on the covered porch, facing the courtyard. I enjoyed practicing Tai Chi on the lush green lawn before breakfast.

On day ten, I woke up at six in the morning and had diarrhea after breakfast. Although I had brought my luggage full of over-the-counter pharmaceuticals, I had neglected to bring anything for diarrhea. Interestingly, the only medicine Kathy brought was an over-the-counter anti-diarrhea medicine. I took a total of three pills and two olive extracts, and drank lots of water. I prayed I would do a quick release and still not miss any part of the trip. And it worked.

I drank more water on our return bus trip to Ollantaytambo, a powerful sacred place where the Sun Temple is located. It's an Incan city where people live in houses built by the original Incas. The Temple of the Condor and the Temple of the Moon are also there. As we climbed the steps of the pyramid, I became nauseated. When we stopped to regain our breath and adjust our energies, I bent over and placed my index and middle fingers in the dirt in front of me to ground myself. The nausea went away immediately.

Looking around, I could see the steep mountains had chiseled faces and staircases. This rock felt as hard as granite. We were told the rocks used for terracing the pyramids were quarried from a mountaintop on the opposite side of the valley, about three miles away.

There were carved niches in the side of the stone walls of the pyramids. We chanted and meditated at each niche, absorbing the healing energies. This whole area was vibrating with a positive and enthusiastic frequency; pure magic and pure love is the best way I can explain what it felt like to be there. Maybe another description that comes close is to say it was like drinking pure, crystal-clear water, quenching a desert-dry thirst.

Willaru gave us a message of encouragement to explore our spirituality and learn as much as we can in this lifetime. "The tree of life or the tree of good and bad. Choose the tree of life and learn more sacred alchemy techniques of the Father-Mother-God."

On day eleven, we left the monastery in our bus and returned to Sacsayhuamán to visit the Temple of the Moon. Willaru performed an official invitation from the Ascended Masters to enter a rock cave housing sacred secret altars. Inside the cave I slipped into a trance. Around me I saw an elephant, a puma, and pyramids. It was so easy to walk across the dimensions and planes of existence inside those caves. I felt safe and accepted by my fellow seekers, our guides, and the *apus* (spirits) inhabiting this rock formation.

I walked by myself over to a massive rock formation that was part of the wall. After I stared at it for a short while, the Masters told me this was a representation of the Akashic records. What I saw in the rock formation was a frontal view of a huge whale. There was a bowl-like depression in the rock at the level of my neck. Bowing with my head forward, I placed the top of my head in the bowl, with my chin resting on my chest. I placed my hands on the two rock protrusions, each about the size of a baseball. These protrusions were at the same level as the depression.

I went into a trance and began speaking the mathematical language. I felt information was being downloaded into me as I felt the energies entering my head and flowing through my body. When the transmission was complete, I walked over to Willaru and told him what had happened. He thanked me for sharing the experience and said he would explore more of it at another time. I encouraged the other women to feel the energy as I did. They each took turns receiving the energies.

We hiked up to the throne of the Inca kings. I meditated, lying on the grass, watching the clouds float by. I was told by the masters that I would feel different when I returned to Phoenix, when my physical body caught up with my light bodies. All was in order. I was not to worry, but just to allow the transition to occur.

When we left for Cusco on the bus the next morning, day twelve, I asked Willaru to speak about the Christ Consciousness and the I AM Presence. I don't remember what he told me because, again, I didn't take notes, and I may have entered into a trance while he channeled the masters. I trust the information is within me.

We arrived in Cusco and checked in to the Cusco Plaza hotel. We returned to our favorite Granja Heidi restaurant, where Thomas, the owner of the tour company, treated us to a free lunch. I enjoyed leek soup, vegetable stuffed peppers, beets, lettuce, potatoes, lemonade, and for dessert, a rice pudding with cinnamon.

We went shopping with Juan in the town. I bought a couple of T-shirts. Kathy and I went for a coffee at a small Chinese restaurant. I love how the world has blended cultures. Now I know why I traveled around the world with Hoyt. Even though it wasn't necessarily a spiritual type of travel, it was for me to experience the food, the environment, the language, and the customs of people, so I would have a greater appreciation of and familiarity with them. The coffee was served in a container, with a separate coffee mug of hot milk. Delicious!

Juan gave Kathy and me written explanations of the Inca ascension cross also known as the Sidereal Year. The cross is divided into four ages: bronze, iron, golden and silver. Each of the ages is also known as a season. Each season is 6,500 years long. Each Sidereal Year or Solar Year is 26,000 years long. In each age, if living unconscious, we live 108 life times before we ascend. We are now in the Iron age just prior to another emerging Golden age.

I bought a hand-knotted floor runner with colorful images of the Mayan calendar. An image of Tumi, the medicine man of the Incas, is woven in multiple images down the center of the rug.

We said good-bye to Willaru in Cusco, feeling blessed by his assistance on our spiritual journey.

The next morning, day thirteen, we flew back to Lima and took a tour of the Museo del Oro, or Gold Museum, to align our frequencies to the ascension frequency of gold—the main purpose of our visit to this museum.

Stacey suggested we not use our brains but just walk into the museum and walk over to a display case. She said, "You will be guided to approach the display of artifacts that resonate with you. There are gold artifacts from different areas of Peru. Just see what happens."

The first part of the museum had weapons. She suggested we not look at the weapons, just keep our eyes down. I didn't mind looking at them because I knew I would be using a sword someday in Tai Chi. The weapons are an energetic form of protection and security for the gold objects.

When I entered the museum, I found myself standing in front of a small display case of gold artifacts from the Nazca area. I laughed. After the Nazca "movie" I experienced, it made sense to me that I would be drawn there. The exhibits of gold glistening under the halogen lights against the black velvet displays were dramatic. I imagined the gold suits of armor were probably ceremonial because gold is a soft metal compared to iron.

We returned to the Hotel Las Palmas in Lima. Alexis and Beatrice left for the airport to return home. Dana treated the three remaining women of our group and Stacey to dinner at the Rosa Nautica restaurant at the end of the pier overlooking the ocean. Our table had red wine and red roses on it. We watched surfers catch the waves. This celebratory dinner was a nice ending to our trip.

Glenda and Kathy left for the airport after dinner. We all hugged each other good-bye, very happy how this tour had evolved. We all felt blessed and changed for the better.

Stacey and Dana left for home the next day at four in the morning. Heidi and I ate breakfast together in the hotel dining room and later took a taxi to the beach. We separated for a little while, meditating by ourselves. I sat under a palm tree and thought of Grandmaster Zaysan. I said to him, *"Z, I wish you were here, experiencing this beautiful place."* I looked up to the sky above me and saw two clouds in the shape of two dragons facing each other—twin dragons. I smiled. He was there in spirit.

The beach didn't have sand. It was full of smooth rocks of different shapes, about two to three inches in diameter. I sat down on the rocks with my legs crossed, and my elbows on my knees, and I asked, *"God, would you give me a remembrance of this sacred trip from nature, that I could take home with me?"* I looked down between my legs and saw a rock the size of a small orange. I picked it up and saw the images carved into it by nature: a puma, an elephant, a llama, a dragon, and a condor. I took this as a sign that I was meant to have it. Still, I asked, *"Is it okay if I take this rock home with me?"*

God said, *"Yes, my child. It is an album of your journey."*

Heidi and I walked to the Mar de Lago shopping mall and ate a leisurely lunch outdoors in a restaurant overlooking the ocean. I thought the dinner we ate the night before was the closure for the trip, but this lunch felt like an extra decompression phase—a soft landing, so to speak. Heidi agreed that we both needed to soak in the warm sun and the gentle ocean breezes before we headed home.

After spending several hours on the beach, we took a taxi back to the hotel and got our bags. We left for the airport a couple of hours early because her flight left before mine. Heidi and I said good-bye in the airport lobby.

I paid the airport exit fee in cash. I checked into my flight at the ticket counter and proceeded to the baggage check. Even though I felt normal, I was in a trance state again. The Peruvian baggage checkers opened my luggage and my carry-on. They sifted through each bag carefully. When they finished, I checked in to my flight, took my carry-on and purse, and sat down at the airport restaurant. I ate my dinner slowly while reading a book.

When I finished my meal, I got up and started walking slowly through the airport, stopping at a gift shop to look at postcards. My waitress came running up to me and said, "You forgot to pay for your meal." I was shocked, and I apologized to her. I had never done that before. I asked her what I owed and gave her the money and a tip. She smiled. She could tell I didn't mean to skip out like that. I probably wasn't the first to do it either.

I boarded the plane and noticed I was one of only two passengers in first class. There was a flight crew headed to Dallas, so they slept in the empty first-class seats. My flight attendant, Genevieve, sat down next to me and asked about my time in Peru. I told her it was a spiritual journey for me. She was a massage therapist and used crystals in her work with her clients. I told her the crystals I purchased in Cusco were in my carry-on bag, and she encouraged me to get them out.

I placed my clear crystal and rose quartz pyramids on the platform next to my seat. Between them, I put a star-shaped clear quartz crystal rock.

When the flight began, I ate a meal and settled back into my seat. Genevieve and I talked for a while, and then I asked if she'd like a blessing and a healing. "Just hold my hands and think of something you would like to be healed within yourself or to receive what would be for your highest and greatest good." I closed my eyes and said a small prayer. I felt the energies rushing through my body and out of my hands. I opened my eyes and nodded. "It is done." She said thank you and returned to her seat.

I stared out the window, looking at the full moon. *"Thank you, God, for this trip, for keeping me safe, and for my return to Phoenix."* I relaxed my muscles and went into deep meditation. I was out for three hours. When I woke up, I looked down at my crystals and realized with some shock that the security people had let me take the large pyramid stone, with its four-inch base, onto the plane. I quickly put them all back in my carry-on. This is when I realized I had been in a trance state.

Genevieve came over and sat down next to me. "I have a message for you, Genevieve. Would you like to hear it?" I asked.

"Oh yes!"

"Stay on your path, and don't look back."

Genevieve's jaw dropped. "Barb, when you gave me that blessing and healing, I walked back to my seat and wrote in my journal. That was exactly what I wrote down."

"Then this is confirmation."

My plane landed in Phoenix at four in the afternoon on Christmas Day. Hoyt picked me up at the airport and drove us to my oldest brother's home for the holiday dinner with my family. Between the jet lag and the energy changes in my fields, I felt like I was in a dream.

This trip to the land of the Incas had been my dream trip. I learned when a person goes on a spiritual trip that emotions and deep-seated issues rise to the surface to be acknowledged and released. My main issue was financial security. I allowed myself an amount to spend and refused to take cash advances from my credit card company—with its 22 percent interest charge. When my fears about having enough money came up, I repeated my affirmation of abundance and trust. And it worked. When I acknowledged and gifted the mother who gave me sacred space and she gifted me with silence, my unexpected reward was a message of security.

I came back to Phoenix with eight dollars in my pocket. The number eight is associated with prosperity, regeneration, the number of sides of the Chinese bagua in feng shui, and the totality of the universe—infinity. How divine.

Chapter 11

MY HEALING GIFT

When I returned from Peru, I assisted a friend undergoing a medical procedure in January, 2005. In the hospital cardiac catheterization prep room, the cardiologist told Joel, "Since you've been a diabetic for ten years, your coronary arteries are probably clogged, and you'll need heart surgery. I have a heart surgeon on standby. See you in a few minutes in the lab." Joel's face tightened, and his eyes searched the room, back and forth, to find comfort.

After the cardiologist left, I told Joel, "Forget everything he just told you." I added affirmatively, "You are going to sail through this procedure with flying colors. You are safe and healthy."

The nurse gave him an oral sedative, and I performed energy healing over his body to calm him while he lay on the gurney. As I placed my hands in his energy fields four inches above his body, tracing his head, arms, chest, abdomen, legs, and feet, he felt the effects of my energy instantly, well before the sedative had time to relax his muscles.

During the procedure, I sat in the large lobby designated for family members and friends to wait while their loved ones underwent heart procedures. I was guided to put the book that I had been reading down on the end table and to stand up and move my body to open up my meridians. I sat back down in my chair with my back against the wall and went into a trance. My body began moving in what would look like convulsions, shaking rapidly as if shivering after a plunge in an icy cold lake, and the fingers of my right hand moved rapidly, hanging toward the floor, so no one could see. (This hand movement is known as weaving. Weaving is a healing modality whereby the practitioner accesses the recipient's energy star fields, manipulating the star codes from disarray to perfect sequences, for optimum health and operation.) I had never done this before. No one in the lobby disturbed me or checked to see if I needed help. When the healing was complete, I came out of a trance and picked up my book and returned to reading.

When the cardiologist came out of the procedure room, he motioned me to step into the hallway and said, "I've never seen this before. I was expecting the narrow, clogged arteries of a diabetic. Instead I saw large, clear arteries. Even if he did have a clot, it wouldn't affect him. And his arteries are clear as a whistle."

When Joel came out of the cath lab, I looked at the black-and-white photo of his heart, showing the dye through the coronary arteries. In the upper left chamber of the heart was a white light in the shape of an upside-down triangle. This is the exact same image I saw through my third eye during the trance. I was inside my friend's heart, not just remotely viewing it.

After this, for weeks, when I drove to work in the morning, I kept asking the same question: *"What did I do in that hospital lobby?"* The answer my angels gave me each time was the same: *"You gave him life."* I didn't understand this.

Three months later, during a private teleconference with Dr. Peebles, I asked, "What did I do for Joel?"

It is not necessary to consciously know what you are doing. The less you know about it, the easier it is to surrender into it. You understand? You did not clear out his arteries. You prevented, during the procedure, him from having a cardiac arrest. You restarted his breathing. He was very, very near to collapse there. His lungs were beginning to fill with liquid. You prevented this from going any further. He had a very, very hard time. He was not willing to surrender, to leave his body during the procedure. He wanted to remain close, and as a result of this, my dear, when you remain close to procedures such as surgery, it can interfere with the process there. It is best when it is a process of complete and total surrender and trust. And so, you see, he was fearful, and he had high expectations, not necessarily of the most positive kind. You disrupted his tendency toward negativity here. You understand? So you saved his life. Yes, absolutely.

I said to Dr. Peebles, "I noticed no one in the lobby was concerned about me and my body shaking, like convulsions."

You helped them to not notice you because they were afraid of you—again, because they just figured best to leave well enough alone. There was, with exception here, a couple who did have, my dear, an awareness that you were a light worker. And that you were doing some very serious work, and they didn't want to interrupt it.

Now I understood what my angels meant by me giving Joel life.

In the first year of Tai Chi classes, I felt self-conscious and stumbled every time Grandmaster Zaysan approached me when I was practicing my form. I imagine this was frustrating for him as a teacher. One time he said to me, "Gee, Barb, I can't even walk up to you and you fall apart." For me, it was like when a basketball player has to make that last basket for the winning point and he "chokes" and misses.

I replied, "I know, Grandmaster Zaysan. I can feel you watching me from across the yard."

I had to learn how not to be affected by what I was sensing. I knew from the beginning that Grandmaster Zaysan could look into my soul. Why would I give this man permission to look this deep inside of me? He could help me in what I needed to learn on the journey to my heart. If I couldn't trust him, who could I trust to help me help myself?

I remember the day I was able to allow Grandmaster Zaysan to watch me and not be so sensitive to it. It was Sunday, the thirteenth of March 2005. When I woke up that morning, my guides told me, *"He's going to push your buttons today."*

I said, *"Okay, I will remember, anything he does 'to' me is just another form of love. I will not be affected by whatever he throws at me."*

I arrived early to class and sat in the yard, talking with Grandmaster Zaysan about truth. I said, "There is truth in everything. Everyone's truth is part of and makes up the whole truth."

He replied, "There is only one truth."

As more students showed up and sat with us, our conversation turned to other subjects. A hummingbird flew in the middle of the group, hovered momentarily, and flew away.

During our warm-up exercises, Grandmaster Zaysan said, "The hummingbird brought a message for someone here. Who was it?" No one spoke.

I hesitated, then said, "It was me." When we completed the warm-up, I told Grandmaster Zaysan, "The hummingbird told me you're going to push my buttons today."

He smiled and put his fists up, pretending he was sparring with me, like a boxer. I thought he was nuts. I knew he could kill me with one punch; I'm only 125 pounds. Why would I fight with him anyway? He's Shaolin, for Pete's sakes! It was just his sense of humor. Thank goodness he was just pretending.

When I walked across the yard and began Form One, I reminded myself to stay centered and unaffected. About halfway through my form, Grandmaster Zaysan walked up behind me, very quietly, and said, "My, that's a nice butt."

Before, I would have stopped my movements, laughed, and told him, *"Stop it!"* Not this time. I figured he was "hitting on" me at my core. I could count on him to use whatever it took to get me to understand and stay centered.

After that comment, in my mind I said, *This is just another form of love.* I felt centered and unaffected. I continued in the form. I could feel his energy trying to push me, to get me to stumble. Not this time. Then he brought out the big guns. He talked about truth, trying to get me to stumble again.

Near the end of the form, I told him with confidence and firmness, "I cannot believe that everything I've experienced is all for naught. This is my truth."

At the end of the form, I stood there feeling unaffected by him. Grandmaster Zaysan became very excited and happy. He said, "You did it!"

"Did what?" I asked.

"You did Form One without falling apart."

I must admit, it was neat seeing him excited and smiling. But I felt this wasn't the end. There would be more lessons, more challenges. Chop wood, carry water. The lessons never end.

During one class, I couldn't stand to be near my fellow students. I was feeling their energy very close to me, and yet they were at least fifteen to twenty feet and more from where I stood. I felt as if I were suffocating.

Grandmaster Zaysan told me, "Go to the other side of the yard."

I was feeling very emotionally upset because I didn't understand why my family had confronted me at the dinner table the evening before. I was trying to understand it, but I couldn't. My family probably didn't even think they were confronting me. It was probably my perception, not theirs.

After working with the other students, Grandmaster Zaysan gave me the ten-pound medicine ball and told me to perform Form One holding the ball in my hands. I was hesitant and didn't understand how to do it.

He said, "Adapt."

I began to move my arms and legs, holding the ball. Within several moves, I became nauseated. I let go of the ball, fell to my hands and knees, and retched. I cried and retched more. When I was done, I stood up.

Grandmaster Zaysan came over and said, "Now, do Form One without the ball."

As I moved, my guides spoke with me. *"Your family is helping you to understand yourself. They are sacrificing themselves so you can learn love; that is how much they love you."* A bubble popped in my mind, a bubble of understanding. I began to cry as I felt even more love for my family and for myself. This is spiritual Tai Chi.

When I learn Tai Chi, I grasp the series of movements in small chunks. Grandmaster Zaysan tries to give me more steps, and I desperately want to be able to perform them, but my brain gets in the way. The brain is a struggle for me. No brain is the answer, but my skull is thick. In the beginning year, I fell down a lot. But I wasn't harmed or bruised because I learned how to fall without hurting myself. I learned how to fall while enjoying it, laughing. Fall down, stand up. Rinse and repeat. It's been nine years now, and I still fall down occasionally. I get up and continue. Just like life. We fumble the ball. We miss an opportunity. Then another comes our way.

I attended Tai Chi classes at different times of the day and at different places: Thursday evenings in the dark with tiki torches on the perimeter of the lawn. Sunday mornings at the temple in the warm sun of summer and the bitter coldness of the night in winter. And Thursday afternoons in a city park. Tai Chi feels different when I perform it in the light of day from how it feels in the darkness of the night. The dark of night provides a closeness to the self. The daylight gives more connection to the Earth because one can see the trees and the blue sky.

I woke up on a Tai Chi class day with a severe muscle spasm in my right upper arm. I had strained my muscles by lifting five-pound weights at home. I couldn't move my shoulder and right arm upward without excruciating pain. Before I went to Tai Chi in the park, I gave myself the option of taking an anti-inflammatory drug for pain and staying home. But I decided to go to Tai Chi without taking the drug. I received a knowing premonition that Grandmaster Zaysan would help me with this pain.

I walked from my car to Grandmaster Zaysan, who was standing next to a picnic table under the pine tree, smoking a cigarette. I put my water bottle on the table and asked, "Can I perform Tai Chi with just one arm?"

He replied with a story of a young man who approached the Shaolin temple in China and asked to come in. The master said he would not let him come in until the snow ran red. To prove his sincerity, the man cut off his left arm. When the master saw the blood in the snow, he let the man in. The one-handed bow we give each other, touching foreheads, is done in honor of this man.

I managed the best I could in the warm-up exercises with the other students, but the pain was almost unbearable. Grandmaster Zaysan helped me in my form by telling me to keep moving. My shoulder muscles burned. At the end of the class, Grandmaster Zaysan placed two of his fingers on the back of my right shoulder and withdrew his hand quickly. I suddenly went into an altered state of consciousness. I couldn't see the trees, the sky, or the ground clearly, so I stood there in a fog.

Grandmaster Zaysan said, "Circle." We walked over to an area under a pine tree and formed a human circle. As we began the cool down movements, voices were fading away. I felt faint. I didn't want to pass out and get bitten by the ants on the ground, so I asked Mother Earth to help me. If I did pass out, I wanted to be able to sit, not lie down. I gave in and let myself pass out. I dropped down to the dirt in a sitting position, with my knees bent and my feet out to one side. I no longer heard Grandmaster Zaysan and the other students talking.

In my third eye, I saw bright-red crystals coming up out of the earth. I let my body fly out to the other side of the universe. I stepped through several triangles of light. Then I slowly returned to my body and consciousness.

I heard Grandmaster Zaysan as if he were talking through a cardboard tube: "Okay, Barb, it's time to wake up. If this isn't exciting enough for you, I can make class more exciting."

I slowly regained consciousness, opened my eyes, and said, "Okay." I stood up. No ant bites. And no shoulder pain. Completely healed and fully conscious. Yes, Zaysan had helped me with my pain.

When I told my massage therapist, Nani, about this healing in the park, she said what I'd received from Grandmaster Zaysan was the equivalent of a one-hour Reiki session in two seconds. "Very few people could handle that type of a healing."

I decided to show up for the Tuesday night class in Phoenix. I wanted to step out of my comfort zone and experience Tai Chi in an unfamiliar place with Grandmaster Zaysan. It was at a two-story home with a backyard of grass, and concrete sidewalks around the front and side. There was only one other student there, a Jewish guy with a golden heart, named John.

Grandmaster Zaysan had us perform our warm-up exercises around the perimeter of the house, moving on grass, concrete, grass, under a tree, between a block wall and the side of the house, forward, backward, and forward again. These exercises felt tougher. The moves were more like kung fu—kicking a leg up in the air, lowering to a squatting position, punching forward with each arm, punching to each opposite side, thrusting a bent elbow, twisting my waist to each side, kicking the other leg up in the air, and repeating these sequences. Sweat poured down the sides of my face. My bra and underwear were wet with perspiration.

Most of the time, it was just this guy and me for class. John exuded great power and direction in his Tai Chi. It was a pleasure to watch him and practice beside him. One time Grandmaster Zaysan had me wear a dry cat-urine-soaked blindfold while performing Tai Chi. The smell was putrid. I could have said no, but instead I decided to see if I could endure the smell and feel the yucky part of this experience while performing the Sword Form. I did it, and afterward there were no untoward effects in me. No infections, no illness.

Grandmaster Zaysan also has classes in a large city park with tall pine trees. My energy expands further in a park. I enjoy Grandmaster Zaysan's style of teaching. He spends a short time with each student, helping each one. I sense he enjoys teaching Tai Chi too. When a student is ready, he gives that student more moves in the form she or he is working on. He moves from one student to the next, showing up at the perfect moment for that student. He reminds me of a kid in a candy store, running from one treat to another with delight. This is the same feeling I experience when I am healing people and teaching. It's pure joy.

One day in the park, when I started Form One, my body began vibrating. I heard a voice just above me say, *"He's going to come over here."* I continued my movements, and then Grandmaster Zaysan came running over to me. He told me to keep going. I completed the form. He told me that when I was about halfway through my form, a white ball of light left my hands when I pushed the energy away. I had been sick with a sinus infection for the previous six weeks. When I finished the form, I was completely healed. He helped me to get rid of what I held on to, which was causing the illness.

When one of us students is moving through emotional challenges, we stay for a little while to talk with Grandmaster Zaysan. With him, one can expose vulnerabilities, disappointments, fears, and frustrations, knowing he has unconditional love. We cry and we laugh as he helps us face our truth. I always leave feeling better and stronger, no matter what I'm processing.

When I was going through a physical change in my body, in one of the Tai Chi classes, I couldn't participate in the warm-up exercises with the other students because I felt resistance and frustration. I stood by Grandmaster Zaysan and watched the other students, who were performing the same movements, all differently. I was surprised. For me, this was confirmation that each student has an individual way of moving his or her body, just like we all have our own way of expressing ourselves and responding to our environment. I then saw how we are helping one another in class. Our collective frequencies help to heal ourselves and one another. I'm grateful for each and every student who shows up at each class, even those who sit and watch, not participating in the movements on the lawn. They still are participating.

One time Grandmaster Zaysan took me too far in the Sword Form. He showed me a new portion of the form, looked at me when I moved my body in the new steps, and said, "Uh oh." He told me not to do that part yet. I didn't understand what he was talking about, until I got home after class. My mind was a mess. I couldn't concentrate and my energy level was very low. At the same time, I could feel Grandmaster Zaysan standing about a foot in front of me. I knew he was protecting me energetically, like a guard. For the rest of the afternoon, all I could do was sit on the sofa watching a NASCAR race, eating a hot dog. It took two days for this state of confusion to leave. I knew I would be okay, so there was no worry on my part. This experience gave me an appreciation of taking my time in my spiritual development. And this applies to everyone. When we are ready, we will proceed on our path accordingly, with grace, joy, and clarity.

* * *

I haven't seen my personal type of healing before. I haven't read about it in any book. When I became aware of the mathematical language, it was difficult to control at times. There were instances when certain people touched me or approached me and the language burst out of my vocal cords. Of course, this startled people, so I quickly calmed them. I had to remind myself that this was in divine order. There's great emotion connected to the language. Slowly, through Tai Chi and energetic adjustments from Grandmaster Zaysan, the Ascended Masters, and others, I began to control the language and keep it within, where it is most helpful for healing people.

I've learned our life on this planet is an unending series of challenges and lessons in learning about love. Even the complicated ones assist us. I've learned to tap into my inner strength and power, deep within me, when I walk through the challenges. I don't require drugs or alcohol to face my fears. I've learned to expect nothing and appreciate everything. I've learned I am blessed. This is what traditional spiritual Tai Chi means to me. I am forever grateful for Grandmaster Zaysan's Tai Chi lessons, healing, and continued guidance.

Chapter 12

REVEALING MORE OF MYSELF

One of my mystical experiences occurred while I was sitting on the living-room sofa making silver-and-glass-bead earrings in the summer of 2002. The doorbell rang on that sunny Saturday afternoon, and I opened the front door. Two women wearing long dresses and holding books and literature began speaking. I instantly recognized these were Jehovah's Witnesses on their mission.

The blonde woman standing closer to me began her introduction after saying hello. "We are here to tell you about how the world is getting worse and going down the toilet—"

I interrupted her speech, but instead of saying I wasn't interested in what she and her friend were offering, I said, "Please excuse me for interrupting you, dear ladies. I am a spiritual teacher and healer, and I must disagree with you. The world is becoming a better place. This is because we all truly love one another and we are One. Thank you."

They looked at me and said, "Thank you," and left.

I closed the door and sat back down on the sofa. An energy transmission started shaking my body like a leaf in the wind. It lasted about ten seconds. A realization came over me, and I ran out the door and down the driveway, and looked in both directions. I could see my neighbors' front yards and entryways to their homes. I didn't see the two women. I knew it would take them some time to walk the front walkway to our driveway, then down the driveway, and across the street to a neighbor's front door.

In other words, these ladies came from someplace else. They didn't have a car; if they did, I would have seen it back out of the driveway and go up the street.

I walked back into the house and asked my guides out loud, "Okay, who were those ladies?"

The answer I received was, *"Archangel Michael and Archangel Gabrielle came to your home to listen to you speak your truth, Dear One. The attunement was their gift to you."*

In 2005, I was given the opportunity to assist a friend who asked me to confirm the Reiki II energy he sent me from more than thirty miles away. He had received a Reiki II attunement in a class that consisted of a short thirty-minute presentation and the attunements. He felt unsure he actually could send Reiki energy. Since I'm sensitive to energies, I offered to be the recipient. We chose a day and time later in the week when I probably would forget about the scheduled "gift." Four days later, while out to dinner with friends, I felt intense waves of soft energy surrounding me. I instantly remembered about the experiment and looked at my watch. It was ten minutes after the time he said he would start sending the energy. I called him and shared the good news.

When I was asked by Berniece, a dear friend who is spiritually open and psychic, to heal her lower back pain, I asked her to stay standing and turn her back toward me. I placed my right hand about one inch from her lower back and spiraled my hand away from her. She was healed instantly.

Berniece had another lower back injury several months later that had kept her home from work for a week. When I found out that she had the injury, I asked her why she hadn't called me to help her.

She said, "Barb, you did help me. I prayed to God to send me an angel to heal my lower back pain. You appeared in my bedroom, and you told me exactly what to do. I followed your instructions, and it worked. My dear, my pain is gone."

At another time, I gave a healing session with Berniece sitting in a chair. I walked around her with my hands about four inches from her head. She said she saw me as an alien, not as a human being. In another healing session on my Reiki table, Berniece saw me change into a Native American male. In that session, I held her hand as she was out of her body, four feet above the table, during one point. When the healing was complete, the sensation of her body returned to the table, and she felt balanced and loved.

I consulted Dr. Peebles again on March 8, 2005. I had more questions, and I wanted to know about my progress in my spiritual lessons. I scheduled another private teleconference with Dr. Peebles, through Summer Bacon.

Dr. Peebles said I had done the unfathomable in this lifetime. I had turned myself completely around. I was not the same person I was yesterday or the day before. I was in a state of constant evolution. Although I was in a period of dormancy, and feeling like I was stuck in quicksand, he recommended I not stress or strain, or I would feel more stuck. He suggested I realize that I am building up strength for a lot of fun down the road. He noted I had nice balance in taking care of myself, being kind to my body, in terms of balancing recreation and work.

I shared with Dr. Peebles that I had been told by spiritual healers and angel communicators that I am a walk-in and a star being from Polaris. He said it was not necessarily confirmed in spirit that I am a walk-in. A lot of what I was experiencing was more from a distant past. As far as being a walk-in in this lifetime, this was more of a memory I was having. I have been a walk-in in a previous lifetime. As far as me being a star being, this is very much so.

Dr. Peebles reiterated I am on earth having a human experience. I had had encounters of all kinds in this lifetime with extraterrestrials. He said I am indeed a light worker and cautioned me not to get too hung up about being strung out about my ego. He reminded me my life is in balance. Dissolving the ego was nothing more than realizing the ego believes it is God. Once the ego understands it is God, it's suddenly free. It's no longer there. It just disappears. The ego can be used for a strengthening perspective about our lives.

I had watched a movie about Joan of Arc, and I felt intense emotions about her. I asked Dr. Peebles if I had a connection to Joan. He replied she was my sister. I had wished that I had the tenacity of spirit that she had. I wished I could have done something to spare her life. In that lifetime, I didn't understand the significance that her burning had for her. She wanted to be burned. She wanted to have that demonstration and be forever etched into the memory of history. However, this did not eradicate the fact that I, as her sister, was incredibly crushed by her disappearance. Joan was my strength, friend, and confidant. She worked very hard to shelter me from the terrors of the day. She felt very much that she was forging a way for me to have a wonderful new future. Unfortunately, for me, it didn't turn out this way. It really ended by messing things up a bit for me. I spent a lot of my life hiding after her passing. The movie had brought up the sincerity of the feelings I would have for a sister. I didn't see her as a figure in history when I was her sister.

When Hoyt and I flew to Europe in May 2002, we visited the town of Rouen, France, where Joan of Arc was burned at the stake in the Old Market Square on May 30, 1431. We went with our friends Maria and Jean-Pierre, who live in Southern France. Jean-Pierre told me the dirt around the site was dug up to bring the soil from the fifteenth century to the top. I felt sad for her death, and yet I felt she accomplished her mission. It wasn't until I had this private consultation with Dr. Peebles that I understood my feelings toward her, and it was one of the reasons I visited Rouen.

I told Dr. Peebles, "As I was returning from Peru on December twenty-fifth, two thousand four, I placed my crystals on the seat console and went into meditation. I have a feeling I was part of the band of energy placed around the planet." He said this was true. I asked again, "Was I specifically off the planet to assist in this band of energy?" He said yes, and that I would be doing this more than just once. It is going to happen several more times in my life because I am a light worker. I am here to do some rather profound restructuring of the planet and helping earth to elevate and such. This comes from centuries of living in the stars and understanding the energy of the star fields.

I shared with Dr. Peebles that my healing abilities have been evolving. I asked if I could teach the mathematical language and my healing technique to others. He said it is not a thing people could easily comprehend at all. It's really something that I have as a natural skill, but for other people, it would take decades to really recreate it. The best they could do is imitating me. This healing is a form of channeling.

I told Dr. Peebles I feel I am a channel for the Light, Love, and Truth of God. He replied, "Exactly!"

It seems people want a quick fix in terms of healing their physical and emotional problems and disease. I asked if this healing I channel will change. He replied that unfortunately, quick fixes are the way of the human being. He shared with me that my healing work will evolve as I evolve.

I had received an e-mail message from a light worker in Florida, warning about a wave of energy coming up from the Southern Hemisphere.

This message was sent to a group of people. We were advised to keep our doors closed and stay away from the south windows of our homes. After reading this e-mail, I said to myself, *What about the people who did not receive this message? What will happen to them?* So, I stood up and performed a light procedure to protect everyone on the planet. Dr. Peebles said it did work because I love everyone very unconditionally.

There are light workers who believe healing can only be done consciously. I asked Dr. Peebles if it matters if I heal people consciously or unconsciously. He said I have no control in that. When I came to planet earth, I chose to not have control. I said, "I am willing to freely heal." I am very much attuned and very much aware of my surroundings at any given moment. Part of this goes to why I tend to not remember the last moment. It's because I'm very aware in this moment. There it goes—now I am in a new moment. I am constantly attuned in perfect alignment, for the most part, with all of the vibrations around me. I can be working very focused on a task, but I am also aware my mind and heart are wandering. I am in mediation at the very same time I'm awake. I have this ability and am very flexible in this respect.

Regarding my spiritual growth, Dr. Peebles recommended more of myself needs to be revealed by bringing more of myself to the surface. This is a never-ending process. There is no "there" to get to. To study the ego is to separate myself out and say it is a bad thing. That I have an ego is not accurate. It is a necessary part. It's the ego that causes a child to start to walk because they feel they can do it. The ego gives you the drive and says you are worthy of something, and there is nothing wrong with this at all. Eventually, a person will fall in love with himself or herself and no longer need the ego anymore. It's a strengthening facet.

Dr. Peebles said that I'm envisioning such things as a Higher Self. He believes there is no such thing. It's only more of who we really are that we are working to access and bring down into our physicality. We are spirits striving to have a human experience.

As far as requiring guidance, Dr. Peebles said I've pretty well figured it out as far as he and his Band of Angels are concerned. I am truly relaxing into my true skin. There are people who will try to muddle the picture for me by saying I am a walk-in, etcetera. That comes off as very lofty and puts me back in my brain. It's important that I am living from my heart space. Once upon a time I did come from the stars, and I was very extraterrestrial in my nature as being very flippant. I was very unemotional in that particular life. I was involved in government, politics, and everything else to try to manipulate the exterior world. Now, in this life, I'm taking that part of myself that really learned to fall in love with planet Earth and now I'm back to create more balance and peace. I still struggle with feeling emotions. I am striving to understand the frequencies of peace, love, and harmony. They are not unimportant. There will be people who will try to make me think they are unimportant because that is their perspective.

In terms of New Age light workers, it's really a matter of old age technology. It's the essence of what began our process on the earth, creating an expansion of God, the desire for Him to breathe life into the earth. Healing is really one of the oldest methodologies around. Instant, hands-on healing came because a person didn't read it in a book. They just felt it in their heart. Everyone then got outspoken and thought they found truth. Truth is just a giant elephant someone grabs by the tail, and says, 'I found it' and someone else grabs by the ear and says, 'I found it.'" There is so much more than that. Everyone's perspective is true to them. It doesn't matter. It can be religious. It can be personal.

Since my last conversation with Dr, Peebles, I've become more forgiving, really forgiving of myself and forgiving of human life around me. I'm not so judgmental. I'm seeing things. No shades of gray now, black or white, or whatever. I do not have the chance to change it, but I can change my perspective of it, inside of myself.

Dr. Peebles said that I was at the crest of my enlightenment. He cautioned me to stop labeling and trying to make it into something because I'm already enlightened. I'm not becoming anything, just revealing more of myself. This is the purpose of my life on Earth. I have integrity and balance. He recommended I not hide myself. I'm not here to slip up. I'm here to learn, to grow, and to expand. He said I will have a deepening of love, and this love is going to hit me hard. This love is going to be an all encompassing sensation of love, but it's going to hurt because it's going to wake me up.

I am here doing God's work, for all humanity. Through my own free will, I chose to find and touch the face of God. I can turn toward thoughts of shame, fear, expectation, melancholy, concerns about disasters, etcetera, or I can choose to be a light worker. I can choose the light from within, who chooses peace over war, intimacy over pain, and who engages in life.

I learned I provide healing for people everywhere I go. One of the quickest healings I observed occurred in a most unexpected place, a hair salon. Gloria, a hairdresser, had recently moved from the East Coast to Phoenix after the deaths of four fellow satanic cult members who committed suicide individually. She felt she was following the same downward spiral of depression and low self-esteem as they had. Her father had recently died too. She was scared she would follow the same path and commit suicide. There was something inside of her that knew she had to leave and start fresh in a new environment if she wanted to live.

As she was shampooing my hair, she told me she understood Reiki healing and felt comfortable talking about spiritual concepts. She also told me about her involvement in worshipping Satan. She no longer wished to be associated with that, but she sensed she still had negative energy and entities around her.

When she finished my hair, I asked her if she would like an energy healing. I told her we could perform the healing right there in the salon, and it would take no more than five minutes. She replied, "Oh yes! I would like that very much."

I invited her to sit in one of the chairs with its back against the wall. I asked her to close her eyes and breathe easily and deeply while I placed my hands around her body, about two inches from the surface of her clothing. I moved my hands around her head, slowly downward alongside her arms and thighs, and down her legs to her ankles and feet. I then placed my hands on her ankles and then on her feet. The energy surged through my body from my head to my feet.

When the healing was complete, I instructed her to open her eyes slowly and become aware of her body. I asked her how she felt.

She said, "I feel good. But Barb, you should see your face."

I turned my head to the left and saw my face in the wall mirror. My skin was the color of a ripe tomato. My hands and arms were normal in appearance. This was odd because I felt completely normal. I advised her to drink extra water that night for the continuation of the healing. I also asked her to write me an e-mail when she felt ready, to let me know how she was doing. I didn't feel any untoward effects while I was in the salon or on the drive home.

When I sat down on the sofa in the living room at home, I sensed a great amount of fear surrounding me. I looked at myself in the mirror in the bathroom and saw my face was still bright red. I walked outside and stood next to the swimming pool and began performing Tai Chi Form One. I sensed a dark entity near me and commanded it to leave me at once. The entity complied immediately. The fear was gone. I went back in the house and saw in the bathroom mirror that my face color was back to normal.

About a month later I received an e-mail message from Gloria. She told me she felt wonderful and her life had turned in a positive direction. She had full-time employment in a beautiful day spa and salon across town. Other aspects of her life had also improved. From the moment of the healing, she no longer felt the satanic energy around her. She felt free.

Her commitment and love for herself, mixed with gentle guidance from the friends who had committed suicide and her father, promoted her healing. This was the most significant part of her healing process. She had taken that big step and moved out of her negative environment. I helped her remove the energetic debris left over from the satanic activities she was engaged in so she could finally raise her wings and gather the wind beneath to soar in her freedom. The rest of her journey is up to her.

Chapter 13

MERGING WITH THE UNIVERSE

I began learning the Sword Form in Tai Chi. In the beginning, Grandmaster Zaysan had me use one of his swords and instructed my fellow students to teach me. The first time I picked up his sword, and performed the honorary bow and blessing to the sword, I heard it speak to me. "Hello, Darling." I giggled. It added, "In a prior life, you swung a Tai Chi sword." In one of the classes at the beginning, the sword took over my control and began swinging in graceful slices in the air. The sword was moving on its own. I could barely keep hold of the hilt and just went for the ride. My body knew where to place my feet, where to jump, and where to turn. The sword took me all over the yard. Conny, who had been practicing near me, stopped her form and sat down on a swing and enjoyed the show. When it was over, I was awestruck and wondered what had just happened. I returned to my form practice and later asked Grandmaster Zaysan about the sword dancing with me. He replied, "It's okay as long as you do it with intention." I walked away wondering what was my intention. I felt I had no say in the matter. The sword had a life of its own.

Grandmaster Zaysan recommended a sword for me to purchase from an online martial arts store. The swords are made in China at a forge called Dragon Well. With the normal nine to ten-day delivery I requested, the sword arrived in three days. Its double-edge blade is twenty-seven inches in length, with a dragon engraved on one side and the sun and moon on the other. The grip is made of hard wood, and it has a large red tassel hanging from the pommel. A pair of dragons facing each other decorates the locket of the scabbard. I felt compelled to sleep with my sword for the first three nights. I brought my new sword to Tai Chi class, and Grandmaster Zaysan blessed it.

The sword is an extension of our energy. I practiced the Sword Form in the backyard. When I moved out of Hoyt's home and into an apartment in October of 2005, I practiced my Tai Chi in a desert park and next to a duck pond with grass.

* * *

In early 2006, I found out I was healing a large number of people on an unconscious level while I was working at an insurance company. During the first two weeks, the chief medical director came over to my desk and said the same thing every day to me: "We're so glad you're here." I voiced my appreciation for being there too. I thought this was a little odd—maybe because I'd never experienced that before or seen this behavior from anyone else at this or other companies I'd worked at.

About four months later, while performing my reviews at my computer, the mathematical language came out of my vocal cords—out loud. I felt I was wrestling with someone. I locked my computer and walked outdoors to a bench, away from other people.

I called Lance and told him what had happened. "This is getting out of control! I can't be speaking this language at work. It would be too disturbing for my coworkers. I don't understand what's happening within me. Do you know what is happening?"

Lance replied, "Everyone in the building is coming to you right now for a healing. You must tell them this is not appropriate. You have computer work to do. You can assign an angel or guide to take reservations so you can heal them later. You must be firm and say the word *no* very loudly in your mind."

We ended our call, and I closed my eyes and focused on this situation. I asked for an angel to be a gatekeeper and take reservations for people who came to me in the physical realm for healing. In my mind, I screamed, *No! I am not available for healings right now. Your desire and need for healing is appreciated. I do love you all. Please see my angel, and she will write your name down. Thank you for honoring my boundaries.*

I opened my eyes and looked up in the sky. I saw a white cloud pattern in the shape of large concentric rings. This was my confirmation that

I had been heard, so I returned to my work. I learned there are times we need to set boundaries and we must honor others' too.

* * *

On April 19, 2006, I underwent hypnosis for a past-life regression with a very gifted hypnotherapist and healer, Cheryl Booth. She is a psychic medium and a compassionate person. I was fortunate to book an appointment with her just before she left for California. After my session, she gave me a CD recording of what I said under hypnosis.

Other than while watching television programs, this was my first time being hypnotized. Under hypnosis, it was revealed that I was a witch in a prior life. This information came through a witch mentor from the 1700s, who spoke through my vocal cords to Cheryl during the regression. I have since heard, from people who understand these matters, many light workers who were witches in a prior life were severely punished and killed for their healing abilities. For those who understand reincarnation, this is why many healers like me have had a struggle exposing ourselves for who we truly are today. It is through healing ourselves our gifts become available. It's safe for us to be who we truly are. Everyone deserves to be healed and guided through the skills and attributes of a psychic healer, if that is their choosing.

Under hypnosis, I also told Cheryl where I go at night. I teach about love when my physical body sleeps. I go to a broadcast station of light and give presentations to large groups of beings on another planet. I have since learned that all humans are assisting others in our dreamtime. All of us go to classes, sometimes to learn and sometimes to teach. I have astral traveled to a spaceship for lessons in the mathematical language running through my body. These lessons took seven years to be fully incorporated into my being on multiple levels and dimensions.

I received confirmation about this language when I tested it with a friend. In March of 2006, Kathy, my friend from Canada, came to visit me in Phoenix. At the time, I was intrigued about the mathematical language I speak. I asked a Chinese woman at the Chinese Cultural Center in Phoenix if the words sounded Chinese to her. She said no, it sounded more like Vietnamese. She recommended I contact someone who is Vietnamese. I suggested to Kathy that we go out to a Vietnamese restaurant and find someone there. I thought bringing a tape recorder would also be helpful.

However, the day before we were going to go to dinner, I said, "Kathy, we don't need to do this. I will find out some other way." I had no conscious idea of what I had just said. Kathy went with the flow and understood we didn't need to test the language at a restaurant.

A couple of weeks before Kathy's visit, a fax machine I'd purchased at an electronics store didn't work when I took it out of the box. I saw that the carbon cartridge didn't fit properly, so I called the manufacturer and described the problem and what I'd found. The woman in customer service agreed that there was a defect, and she told me she would send a new cartridge with the correct part by mail.

After two weeks and no part in the mail, I called customer service again. I was told there was no record of a complaint from me in their system. An easier path to solve this problem seemed the best way for me, so I said, "Okay, I will take it back to the store and exchange it for a new one. This store is known for its superb customer service." The rep on the phone agreed.

Kathy and I went to the electronics store, and I checked in at the return counter. There I received a piece of paper confirming I had brought something into the store for an exchange. We walked over to the computer section of the store just to see what was new in computers.

As we walked around the counter, Kathy pulled me aside and said, "Barb, those two guys over there are talking the same language you speak."

I said, "Okay, let's do an experiment and see if they recognize the language. I'll pretend I'm talking to you, and I'll speak the language, and you just nod your head in agreement." When we did this, the guys didn't even notice or recognize I was speaking a foreign language. I told Kathy, "Oh well. Let's go get the fax machine."

When we walked up to the fax machines next to the side wall of the building, I noticed a thin Asian man standing in front of models like the one I had purchased. I acknowledged his presence, then took a boxed fax machine and put it in my cart.

When we started to walk away, Kathy said, "Barb, you just missed an opportunity."

I looked at the guy and then at Kathy and said, "No, I didn't. Come on."

We walked up to the Asian guy and I asked him, "Excuse me. Are you Vietnamese?"

He said, "Yes."

"Well, I speak a language, and it sounds Vietnamese. If I speak a little of it, would you tell us if it is indeed Vietnamese?"

He agreed. After I spoke a couple of "sentences," he said, "No, it's not Vietnamese. It's for healing and for protection." His answer was spoken in a respectful and gentle tone. We both thanked him for his help, and I asked him for his name. He replied, "Mike."

When Kathy and I walked back to the return counter, the clerk asked me to show him what was wrong with the fax machine I'd brought in. I took the machine and the parts out of the box and began to install the cartridge. About halfway through this process, I received information in my mind: *This cartridge will fit perfectly.*

I started laughing. And when it set into the machine as it was designed, I looked up and told Kathy, "That guy was Archangel Michael. If we walk back to the fax machines, he won't be there."

Not only was this experience a message to me about communications with our angels, it is an example of how a mystical experience can happen in our ordinary life. It kind of makes you stop and slow down in your daily interactions with people and realize you may very well be speaking with an angel. What I find interesting and humorous is the many ways our angels communicate with us—or should I say, how we create the journeys to find the answers to our questions. I even looked up first names for Vietnamese boys. *Mike* is not a common name for people of Vietnamese descent. Vietnamese people name their male babies with a positive characteristic, such as *An*, for peace or peacefulness, or *Minh*, meaning "bright."

* * *

On June 6, 2006, Hoyt and my dissolution of marriage petition was signed by a judge. I continue to be friends with Hoyt, and I still speak highly of him. He is a good man. He has made profound contributions to our global society in computer communication security standards and electronic commerce processes. He continues to be a role model in respecting and caring for all animals and sentient beings. Hoyt saves bees from drowning in the swimming pool and feeds and cares for stray cats.

I have much to be grateful for in my marriage and my relationship with Hoyt. If it weren't for his sacrifice, I would not have sought and walked the spiritual path to leave him.

Healing opens our awareness of our experiences. We're going to have experiences, whether we are aware of them or not. With a greater awareness, we begin to experience the negative ones with a fresh, positive perspective. Even though it doesn't feel positive, there is some degree of change in us.

In a meditation in the citrus garden, my angels told me I was the one instructing other people to behave and communicate messages to me— good or bad. This is all part of my experiences on planet Earth. I now understand that this concept mirrors the idea that the people in my reality are a reflection of me. This means I must take ownership or responsibility for my reality. Everything that has happened with me is my creation.

I had my last private teleconference with Dr. Peebles and the Band of Angels on April 5, 2006.

I shared with Dr. Peebles about the fax machine and Archangel Michael story. I asked him his opinion about the mathematical language. He replied that the Vietnamese guy at the electronics store was indeed Archangel Michael. However, the language was not necessarily for protection, but for healing and other purposes. Sometimes my clients are so tired and frustrated and they come to me very angry. They are not willing to make a connection with me. They expect me to make the connection with them. It's similar to speaking in tongues. There are spirits that have specialized in charging a room with energy and are willing to bring about the connection between myself and my client. It's like playing beautiful music while I work.

I said to Dr. Peebles, everyone has brought a gift to Mother Earth that enables them to heal themselves and others. It is just a matter of opening up the package that is their true self. Is this your understanding as well? Dr. Peebles replied, yes, and it's a matter of saying yes to it. That is the hardest part for anyone to do. It's about giving and receiving abundance here and saying, yes, I know what I have, and I know what I can give, and I'm going to do it. It's frightening for most human beings, so they will find any way not to do what they came here to do. It's frightening to understand your own power. It's really simple. It's the awareness all of life is an energy. It's nothing you have to find outside of yourself. It's already there. It's also very hard to release expectations and to surrender to that truth.

I shared with Dr. Peebles that I took the meditation I did since I was seven years old one step further. What if there is no love? Is this possible? He replied, *It's impossible. The best you can do is hold it at arm's length. But the truth is, love never disappears entirely. We can squash it as small as we can, but there will always be a grain of sand on the shore of love. This is the truth.*

I asked Dr. Peebles about the attunements I receive from the Ascended Masters. I feel as if I am downloading information into my essence when

I read certain statements, such as in books. My whole body shakes when I read a passage or concept. He said the downloading of information is exactly what I'm doing during the attunements and in my reading. I don't like to regurgitate what I read; however, there are things that need to be in my consciousness, so that when it's time, my guides can speak this truth to someone. The attunements and the downloads are charging me up, giving me the tools and phrases that I need to understand later when I'm healing and guiding people.

I shared with Dr. Peebles, a dream, that I saw myself in the mirror, looking like an alien. I wondered if this is one of my states of being. He replied in the affirmative. I wanted to know the purpose of me being an alien. He said that an alien is God too. My biggest mission on Earth is to bring love to the world. I'm to learn about love, appreciate it, and bring it back to a group of extraterrestrials who do not understand it. I'm here in exploration. Because I'm part of this alien being, I have a personality that tends to be a bit detached. This trait helped me to be calm while working in intensive care as a nurse. It's not that I'm unloving, just not attached to anything too much. I shared with Dr. Peebles I don't want to get into dramas with people. He said that I have a beautiful balance in this, and I'm teaching others on the planet to have this personality trait. The alien culture I come from is called Zagian. Zagians are very female, very feminine, and balanced in the male and female energies. This is one reason why I have a take-charge personality.

This channeling was the first time I heard the name of the ETs I come from, the Zagians. What I appreciate is that the Zagians may not understand what love is, so they sent me to Earth to learn about love and to teach them. It's amazing to me that a group of beings on another planet is eager to learn about love from our lovely planet Earth.

One Sunday afternoon, in May of 2005, I came home from tai chi and sat down with my lap top computer on the sofa. I started writing in my journal. All of sudden, the letters of the words I had just typed, fell down the page all by themselves, into a pile and disappeared from the document page. A geometric pattern formed on my computer document screen. It was shaped like a slice of pie and there were several geometric patterns. I put the computer down on the coffee table and moved my arm out to my right side. My arm disappeared. I ran to the bathroom and stood in front of the mirror. When I turned my head to the left a couple of degrees, my image in the mirror disappeared. This all lasted about twenty minutes. I wasn't taking any drugs. I knew I wasn't hallucinating from dehydration. I asked Dr. Peebles about this phenomenon. He said I was dissolving illusions of barriers, borders, and boundaries. It was like a trance state. I was seeing different dimensions. I was looking at myself days ago standing in front of the mirror—all of it existing at one time. I merged with the universe for a moment. I sent Grandmaster Zaysan an e-mail message about this experience just after it happened. He replied that I had tasted mindfulness. I had a whopping headache for twenty minutes afterwards. Although the experience was "cool," I didn't like the headache part.

Dr. Peebles felt at this time on my spiritual journey that I am compassionate. Patience was the next big lesson. It was important that I slow down and take time to listen to everything and everybody, especially the items around me. This training was to teach me about hearing into other dimensions and seeing the light that is there.

Over the four years I embraced Dr. Peeble's teachings and spiritual guidance through channelings, books, classes, and seminars, I noticed more often than not that I quoted him when I spoke with people and my clients. I came to a crossroad in the summer of 2006: a need to define my own spiritual self. For me, this meant I had to say good-bye to Dr. Peebles. I spoke with him about this, and he graciously agreed. This also means I was separating Dr. Peebles from me, but if we truly embrace the oneness, there is no separation. Rather, it must be a concept we use when we decide to speak and embrace our own truth. It is possible that my entire experience with Dr. Peebles was to bring me to this moment of deciding I must trust in myself and speak from own heart. If I am to acknowledge and embrace all perspectives, then I cannot follow any one particular religion or guru.

I am grateful for the experience of talking with Dr. Peebles and receiving healing from his Band of Angels, including Jesus Christ. I am also grateful for Summer Bacon's and Ann Alber's ability to trance channel. Summer shared with me after my first private teleconference that she experienced a very warm and loving feeling while she was in the trance state. Only she knows what this meant for her. I love Summer and Ann very much.

Through the information gathered in the three private sessions with Dr. Peebles, I was able to see several benchmarks in my spiritual growth and begin to grasp the magnitude of this gift from God that flows through me to help people on their journey. I still have more lessons to learn and information to understand.

Chapter 14

THE CAT'S MEOW

One evening in July of 2006, at about ten o'clock, I carried my kitchen garbage bag from my second-story apartment downstairs to the community Dumpster on the west side of the parking lot. I felt the hot summer air on my face and arms. It was breezy too. Lightning flashed in the distant sky from a brewing monsoon storm.

About ten feet from the trash Dumpster, in a storm drain runoff area, gazing at the stars with his back toward me, lay a gray-and-black, tiger-striped cat on the rocks. He turned his head, and I said, "Hi there. You must be thirsty in this heat, 'cause you're panting."

I threw the bag in the Dumpster, walked back to my apartment, and brought back a plastic container of water with ice cubes, shallow enough for a cat to drink without straining his neck. I noticed he didn't have a collar.

"There you go. You're a nice kitty." I walked back to my apartment, and he followed me up the stairs and into my living room.

He snooped around like a security guard on duty, checking each room, and finally sat down in the kitchen. I called Hoyt and asked for a favor. I drove over to his house and picked up a small litter box, litter, and dry food for my furry guest.

Now, my dilemma was whether to meet an obligation to a hospice volunteer training course I was enrolled in at the time or return the cat to its owner. That night I woke up and saw large energy waves rising from the cat's body. The waves were flowing toward the walls and ceiling as he lay on his back, asleep on my bed. He looked so comfortable and safe, and I sensed he was a master. I fell back to sleep.

In the morning I left the cat at the Humane Society, thinking the owners might be looking for it there. But then I thought, *Why didn't I just leave the cat alone? Why did I get involved? Wait a minute. He followed me home. I didn't pick him up and carry him against his will. But now I'm involved.* I felt a sense of obligation to find his owner, so I blew off the hospice volunteer training and canvassed the neighborhood behind my apartment. One man told me this feline was the terror of the neighborhood, picking fights with other cats, and no one liked his whiskers snooping around their yards.

I found the home where this cat lived (according to other neighbors), but nobody was home. I left a note taped to the front door, explaining what I had done and asking them to contact me through my cell phone number. That evening the woman whose house I had left the message on called me and said she didn't own the cat. I was a little surprised, after what her neighbor had told me. But maybe it didn't matter. The big picture was that I knew this cat chose me to care for him, and I had accepted this stewardship by inviting him into my home.

I bought a cat carrier and a larger litter box, the kind with a cover and charcoal filter to cut down on odors. I drove to the Humane Society, thinking I could bring him home that afternoon. Boy, was I wrong.

The Humane Society has a protocol designed to protect the best interest of pet owners and their furry friends. Animals brought in are "quarantined" for three days to make sure they are free from diseases like rabies. Plus, this gives people a chance to check whether their lost pet found its way to the place where animals hold reunions, or allows the animal to be adopted by someone else. Sadly, some, if not many, are euthanized. I felt disappointed that I couldn't take the cat home. But I decided to turn the situation into a positive one.

I brought homemade desserts to the caretakers at the facility. They let me walk back to where the cats were in cages. Each time he saw me, he went to his food dish, communicating his happiness. I held him each day for a short time, and we bonded. I could hear the other cats communicating with this cat, whom I now called Galileo because he was looking up at the stars when I first laid eyes on him. I think it's a noble name for a cat, especially this one.

"Thank you for bringing her here," the other cats said. While this surprised me, I understood that Galileo and I were meant to stand in the middle of that housing area with all the caged cats around us, while a healing was channeled for everyone. The employees understood what I was doing and allowed me to hold him. I sadly said good-bye each day, but knew we would be together once the quarantine period was over. I told him so too.

I came back on the fourth day, paid the fees, completed the forms, arranged for a security deposit and rent charges with my landlord, and brought Galileo home in the new carrier.

I was no longer by myself. I now had a new member in my home. We had become a family of two. Felines are nocturnal. Every morning around 3:00 a.m., Galileo wanted to go outside. It was difficult to refuse his unrelenting request, but I knew we would make it. I told him just two more months, then we would be moving to a home where he could go outside and play. I carried him to the balcony each night and held him, showing him the hot night air, the stars, and how much I cared about his safety. I couldn't let him jump from the second-story balcony. After communicating his disappointment with cries, eventually he went back to sleep, and so did I.

I bought cornmeal litter so Galileo would have a natural, organic place to potty. When I took him to my vet and had him examined, it was discovered that he had an infected tooth. He must have been in misery, but he never showed it—at least not to me. My vet put him under anesthesia and removed the infected tooth. We noted Galileo had front teeth missing, too, probably because of his rough kittyhood.

He had the most beautiful fur coat design. I loved practicing my Tai Chi and meditating, with my eyes half closed, on the design of his fur glistening in the sun. It was very pleasing to gaze on the light and dark stripes. Galileo's turquoise eyes spoke tenderness and love to me. He called me "Mama" when he spoke to me telepathically.

Finally, on September 14, 2006, we moved to our new home in Peoria. I remember when I let him outside for ten minutes, he came right back in. The next time I let him out, I watched as he walked around to the neighbor's driveway. I thought he had walked too far, so I picked him up and carried him back to our yard. When the metal gate closed behind us, it caused a loud noise, startling him. He flew out of my arms. I touched the blood dripping down my cheek from his sharp claws as I said, exasperated, "Fine, you know what's best!" An hour later, Galileo was sitting at the sliding glass door, wanting to come in. I was so happy he had returned. I was the one who had to learn he could be trusted to go outside.

Galileo communicated to me through his body language too. One evening I came home by myself from eating dinner with a friend at a Chinese restaurant. I had just moved into my new home. When I opened the front door, my cat, Galileo, was running around inside the house like a headless chicken. I felt a prickly sensation on the back of my neck. I saw that one curtain in the guest bedroom was hanging down instead of tied back. I knew it would have been very difficult for Galileo to untie the knot that I had secured in the brass hook in the wall. In fact, he never bothered any of the tiebacks in the house before and after this event.

I could sense negativity in the house. I told Galileo, "Calm down. I will take care of this." He responded to my instruction immediately and strolled into the master bedroom and lay down on the bed. Although I could not see the spirits in my home, I spoke firmly and directly, "This is a home of peace, love, harmony, and compassion. If you cannot behave in this manner, then you must leave now." I didn't have anger or fear toward the spirits in the house.

I heard someone say reluctantly, "Okay." The vibration in the house returned to normal. I put the curtain back in place and smudged the house with sage.

One of my fondest memories of Galileo was when he would stand on my chest while I massaged his armpits with my thumbs. His purrs confirmed his pleasure. After the massage, he would lie down on my chest as I stroked his soft fur and petted his head. I loved it when we napped together quietly in the afternoons. I enjoyed seeing him asleep on the sofa or on the bed, curled up, with his head upside down, deep in dreamland. This was always a comforting image for me, a reminder that all is okay with the world. Nothing else matters.

I set up Galileo's food and water in the kitchen, under the breakfast bar. He would never eat meat or fish, only dry cat food. However, he loved the melted butter on my breakfast plate and the vanilla yogurt from my bowl in the evening.

Galileo was a good kitty. He never disturbed my porcelain dolls' dresses or attacked their mohair wigs. He respected my stuff. He would lie down and sleep while I worked on my computer or watched a program on TV. I loved how he tucked one front leg under his chest and stretched the other front leg out over the sofa.

One time he brought a lizard in the house. It ran up the sofa, into my bathrobe, up my neck, and flew across the room from my thrashing arm as I screamed, "Galileo!" Laughing, I told him, "This lizard is not a pet!" He looked at me with an "uh-oh, what did I do?" look on his face. We found the lizard the next day and put the little reptile outside.

Galileo was the best kitty. When I worked Monday through Friday during the day, he slept and held down the fort. He greeted me when I came home, then went outdoors to potty. He preferred to do his business outdoors instead of in the litter box. He came back in for dinner and our quiet time together. He hung out with the four cats that live next door to us.

When it was time for my bedtime, Galileo went outside. Several times during the night, he would scratch the sliding door window or cry to be let in. From my bed, I could hear his meows easily. He enjoyed going outside several times while I slept. I would get up, let him in, and return to bed and fall right to sleep. We did this several times during the night, and I didn't mind until it happened five times in a row. We found my limit of being awoken by a cat. This was the only time I complained about this repetitive procedure. Perhaps another person would remark I spoiled this cat or that the cat dominated me. And yet, this simple act of Galileo crying to come in and to go outdoors, served to give me a metaphysical experience. One night, when he sat outside the sliding glass door next to my bedroom, crying to come in, I could feel his meow sound travel through the stucco wall, enter my room and everything in that moment, merged into one. I was awake and feeling complete oneness with all objects, sounds, words, concepts, life, everything. It was a beautiful feeling. This oneness lasted about twenty seconds.

I loved Galileo very much, and I told him every day. He was very generous in helping people to heal when they came to our house for a healing session on the Reiki table. He would jump up—with my client's permission, of course—and lie down on the area of the body that needed healing. When he was done, he jumped down and walked out of the room. I was very grateful for his assistance. I had a great respect for his method of healing, and my clients enjoyed his healing technique too.

Fairies inhabited my house in Peoria, and Galileo confirmed their presence. When I held him in my arms at home, he twisted his head around, watching the fairies darting around the room. In the northwest corner of the breakfast room, Galileo stood on the china cabinet, staring up toward the ceiling, standing on his hind legs with his front paws on the wall, talking with the fairies passing by. I understood that this area of the kitchen was a portal, or gateway, for the fairies.

Galileo ran around like a crazy chicken when someone approached the house with intense chaotic energies. This helped me to understand what energies a person was bringing to the house. As soon as I said, "Okay, I got it," Galileo would settled down.

Chapter 15

SPIRITUAL BOTOX

In 2007, a medical aesthetician named Chloe asked me to join her in opening a new medical spa across town. I was already seeing my work at the insurance company coming to an end. When the computer program I used to perform my job began to act in a bizarre manner and other signs presented, I knew it was time to leave. My two managers had already left the company. If I were meant to stay there, the signs of support would have been felt, without a doubt. So I left.

Entertaining the idea of self-employment without a steady paycheck in an arena where I hadn't been before left me struggling with how I was going to pay my mortgage, utilities, and insurance premiums. If I took the leap into owning a business without another income, I would be trusting the universe about financial support. I felt scared about venturing out on my own, and Chloe felt my concerns too. Plus, I had to provide food and shelter for Galileo.

Even though I had my 401(k) and stock investment fund as a backup, I felt I should have an income from a steady job too. In addition, I needed to be trained in cosmetic Botox and dermal filler injection techniques. I didn't even know if I would be competent in these procedures. But the idea of being my own boss and providing services to people sounded appealing.

Even Chloe gave me a hard talk about being sure and confident in going into business alongside her. We agreed each of us would be operating independently yet referring customers to one another. She had a proven track record with a lucrative aesthetic business. Surely, between the two of us, we could have a successful medical spa. Those around us agreed. Now it was a matter of combining our synergy in creating a successful spa with safe practices. We had the incentive and the knowledge to make it happen. We were also applying the law of attraction and abundance. So it was a no-brainer that it was time to jump in.

Chloe arranged for me to receive training from a certified Allergan injector nurse trainer in Phoenix. Allergan is the company that distributes cosmetic Botox in the United States. Cosmetic Botox is different from medical Botox used for dystonia conditions such as torticollis. The cosmetic version is used to relax the muscles under wrinkled skin, producing a softer and younger appearance.

After a concentrated week of study, I performed injections on live models, including the medical director for our medical spa. I also received the cosmetic Botox and dermal filler injections by the trainer so I would know what it feels like and experience the aftercare and changes in my muscles and skin. The trainer observed I had a delicate touch when I injected the products, and several of the models said they couldn't feel the needle in their skin. I felt this was due to the extremely small diameter of the needle and my steady hand.

After the performance portion of the class, I was excited about going further with this venture. I could see providing these services with integrity and combining them with my healing and teaching gifts. I was excited about working with a medical aesthetician who held the same philosophy about professionalism, ethics, and business that I did.

The medical spa was located inside a day spa and salon. Chloe had her movers deliver her stored spa furniture. I ordered the signs for the doors, decorated the spa, and purchased a couple more pieces of inexpensive furniture for my treatment room.

We hired a feng shui practitioner to promote success and well-being for our clients in the med spa. The practitioner helped us in placing the furniture and decorative objects in the right places to facilitate an auspicious energy flow through the rooms. We performed a manifesting ceremony and prayed in our treatment rooms for our clients' safety, honor, well-being, and healing. The feeling in the med spa was feminine, soft, and peaceful.

Before she left, the feng shui practitioner pulled me aside and said, "You understand, she [Chloe] will not be here very long."

Without even thinking about it, I replied, "Yes, I know." I'd had a feeling this adventure would be changing and requiring more from me than I had anticipated, but I was still willing to experience it.

I created a limited-liability company with the help of my attorney, and Chloe and I signed a month-to-month lease with the salon owners. I set up my account with Allergan so I could purchase the products through my medical director's DEA license, and I followed the state health guidelines for setting up a treatment room and the protocols for sterile and clean procedures and proper hazardous waste disposal.

Brochures and business cards were printed. We created advertising incentives to promote clients. I sat down with the hairdressers, cosmetologists, and other aestheticians working in the day spa and salon, and developed a referral arrangement to draw more customers to the salon and med spa.

I was excited and ready to open my practice on December 1, 2007. But the night before the opening, the medical director called to say he didn't want to accept the liability as my supervising physician. I told him I understood the risks involved for him, and I wished him well. Without a medical director, I couldn't touch a client and start my business; the Arizona Nurse Practice Act stipulated that I must have a medical doctor review my documentation and sign my client files. So I began a search for a new medical director. I quickly found out the doctors who were offering themselves in this position were commanding $3,000 a month from aesthetic nurses. The medical spa corporations could afford this fee, but I couldn't. It was way out of my budget.

I made an appointment with a successful dermatologist in Scottsdale to seek his advice. He sent his representative to my office to make sure I was "legit" and serious about the business. The representative also checked to make sure the treatment rooms and the office were clean and properly set up; otherwise, no meeting would occur. I imagine there are all kinds of med spa offices that aren't up to standards, just as those found in other businesses. I was happy to have the critique. A confirmation of the appointment with the dermatologist meant I had passed the inspection.

The dermatologist graciously gave me a tour of his beautifully appointed office. I saw a man receiving hair transplant plugs in one room. The other treatment rooms were empty since it was after five in the afternoon. We sat in his private office, and he told me the ins and outs and the pros and cons of operating an aesthetic practice in the Phoenix area. He tried to discourage me from operating on my own with a medical director who didn't have expertise in the procedures or who was unfamiliar with potential complications.

I searched for a month. I found a doctor who agreed to be my medical director. His specialty was OB-GYN. My injector trainer was an aesthetic nurse who provided her services inside an OB-GYN medical office.

Everyone has angels and guides on the other side helping them in their professions, hobbies, and day-to-day activities. So I asked God to send me a specialist angel medical doctor on the other side to assist me. The angel doctor came to me instantaneously. He introduced himself as Dr. Mark. In his prior life, he was a plastic surgeon on the East Coast. He told me he would watch over me and assist in my aesthetic practice.

My new medical director and I met for coffee in Phoenix to talk about the procedures for his supervision of my practice. He also is a spiritual person and receives information from the angelic realm.

When we concluded our conversation, he said to me, "And, Barb, when it's time to get out of this business, it's time to get out. Do you understand what I mean?"

I sensed he was foretelling something. I understood what he was telling me to be the truth and for me to pay special attention to his warning. "Yes, I understand."

Now, my director had to receive the same training I went through. We arranged for his class instruction, and I participated in giving some injections too. I began accepting clients in the beginning of February 2008.

Chloe brought her previous clients to our medical spa for services, including cosmetic Botox. She gave microdermabrasion treatments and facials with a beautiful, angelic healing technique. She was well known as an angel communicator and used this gift to guide her clients in their personal and professional lives.

The cosmetologists and I hosted a couple of spa events with door prizes for reduced or free services. Participants received ten-minute introductory services like massages, mini-facials, hair restyling and consultations, mini-manicures, and demonstrations of permanent makeup. Most of the women who came to the spa events weren't interested in my aesthetic services, but two asked to receive angel communications and healing energy. I gave them half-hour sessions.

When I began giving cosmetic Botox injections, the medical standard for the refrigeration shelf life of the reconstituted drug was a matter of days. If I didn't have enough clients to use up the Botox, I had to dispose of it in a hazardous waste container, throwing out as much as $600 of product at a time. To me, this was insane. About a month later, Allergan came out with a new protocol, allowing the mixed Botox be kept refrigerated up to a month and still be potent to facilitate muscle relaxation. This meant I no longer had to dispose of unused product that was not expired.

I embraced my instructor's guideline in educating people in the proper dosages and time frames for Botox. As I talked with clients about the cosmetic Botox they'd received from other med spas, it became apparent many were receiving a very diluted form. I was hearing things like "You can have as much Botox as you want and as often as you want." This is not how cosmetic Botox was designed to work and could possibly lead to bad side effects. I shared the information I was taught and let the clients make their own informed decisions.

I received more requests for healing than for aesthetic services. One afternoon, a mother and her two adult daughters came to the medical spa inquiring about Botox and dermal filler products. They sat down with me in the office, emanating a sweetness in their personalities. The conversation turned quickly to metaphysical and spiritual concepts. I spoke the language of the heart to the point that tears rolled down their cheeks. I spoke about compassion, forgiveness, and allowing people to be who they are. I interwove these concepts with stories and tied it into the Botox and dermal filler information. After two hours, we said good-bye. I walked out to my car not understanding what was happening to me. I saw myself more as a spiritual teacher than as an aesthetic nurse.

One evening while I was sitting in the medical spa by myself, a Brazilian woman walked in. She said, "Hi, I was guided to come here. I don't know why. So here I am."

I invited her to sit and visit with me. She didn't even know she had walked into a medical spa. I told her about the services the aesthetician and I provided. Then we spoke about spiritual matters instead.

I did my best to explain my type of energetic healing, and then she asked me, "Do you know João de Deus [John of God]?"

I had heard of him, but I was not aware of his specific healing technique.

She said, "He's in Brazil. You are healing people in the same way he does."

"People don't have to go to Brazil for the healing."

This is when I realized she had come to me for a healing and to impart information. We held hands while I entered a state of altered consciousness. She said she could feel the energies flowing from my hands into her body. She gave me her business card, thanked me, and left the office.

When I returned to my home, I looked up John of God on the Internet. I went to his website and saw he was using physical instruments inserted through the nasal cavity and into the brain of people suffering from cancer and other ailments. These techniques are guided by physicians on the other side.

A client, Celeste, who was forty-one and understood spiritual concepts, came in one evening for Botox injections. We sat in the office while she decompressed from her worries. Celeste shared with me that she had lost her job and was very concerned about how she was going to pay her bills. She had hired a career consultant to help her find employment. I understood her desire to look as fresh and young as possible since she was competing with younger job seekers.

We walked back to my treatment room, where the lights were dimmed to facilitate relaxation and healing. After the usual hand washing and blessing, I moved my hands in the air, just over her body, giving Celeste an energetic form of light anesthesia. With my hands over her body, I channeled the healing. While I was in an altered state, I watched her face become twenty years younger. I had not even given her the Botox yet. After the healing session, she was sufficiently relaxed for me to give her the injections. The wrinkles returned before my eyes, and I gave her the cosmetic Botox. She said she barely felt the needle, and I shared with her the earlier transformation I had witnessed in her face.

Two weeks later, I called Celeste to check on the effects of her treatment. Excited, she shared with me what happened the night I gave her the injections. She had left my office, walked out to her car, and received a phone call with news of a job offer from a former employer she had worked for twenty years ago. The transformation message I received during the healing was about her new job! She was happy and relaxed.

I performed a healing of another woman in 2008, who didn't know she had been abused sexually when she was younger; she had repressed the memories. When I asked her what the extra fat tissue around her waist was for, she saw a vision, and she remembered. Tears flowed, and she was released from her childhood trauma. The next time I saw her, she was glowing with happiness. Her smile expressed her freedom. And when I saw her out in public, she continued to express her happiness and gratitude for the healing.

By June, I still wasn't making enough money to pay my part of the mortgage, utilities, and rent at the spa. I had already pulled money from my stock fund to pay my parents back on a loan, so I withdrew from my 401(k). I called the credit card companies and my mortgage lender to negotiate to decrease my payments, but no one would work with me. Soon the automated phone calls from the collection agencies began. I learned to avoid answering the phone, allowing the answering machine to take the messages. When the phone calls from the bill collectors increased, I blocked them.

I couldn't afford the $300 early return fee for the credit card service at my medical director's office. The man in charge of this service waived the fee for me. He understood my position, because he had been through a personal bankruptcy. He demonstrated compassion for me.

I didn't see much of Chloe because she was going through a similar situation, and on top of that, she was in the middle of a child custody battle. By the end of June, she closed her business. She had tried her best to find clients, but the flow of money never manifested. She moved her business and furniture out, so I purchased an inexpensive, slightly damaged desk and decorated the spa with items from my home, creating a Hawaiian decor.

One of the owners of the day spa and salon suggested I go with another aesthetician from our day spa to gentlemen's clubs in Phoenix and market our services to the women who worked as topless dancers. Some dancers used cosmetic Botox to maintain their youthful appearance. Each time I had asked the aesthetician about going with me, she had other commitments. One Saturday afternoon, the owner told me, "Go now."

I drove directly to a club in northern Phoenix. Before I went in, I sat in my car, scared. *Why am I scared?* I asked myself. *Look, you are making assumptions about how you will be received by the people inside this club. Isn't it time to stop making assumptions?* I replied to myself, *Okay, let's drop these judgments. I don't know these people, and for all I know, they could be really down-to-earth, nice people.* I took a deep breath, gathered my brochures and business cards, and jumped out of my car.

I walked into the club, and it took a few moments for my eyes to adjust to the darkness. I walked past the bar and sat down in a corner with a sofa and end table. A middle-aged couple watched a topless black-haired woman dancing around a silver metal pole on an elevated platform surrounded by black lights. I ordered an Amaretto and Coke and sipped it while I got my bearings. No one approached me. Men at the bar turned their heads to look at me, but they didn't remove themselves from their beers. I was glad they stayed away from me; I wasn't there to be picked up.

When the dancer left the small stage and the black lights turned off, I walked over to another part of the club where a larger stage and more chairs with tables offered more customers the opportunity to watch a parade of topless dancers. I noticed the dancers were young, except for one middle-aged dancer with a body build similar to mine. This sort of shocked me because it was like looking at myself. I couldn't imagine dancing topless in front of people. I felt like a fish out of water here.

When I finished my drink, I walked over and asked the bartender if I could speak to the general manager. I was told to return on Monday in the afternoon. I thanked him and left feeling optimistic with my introduction to the topless dancing environment.

I returned the following Monday. The general manger was very cordial and receptive about the services I offered. He encouraged me to leave my brochures and business cards in the dressing rooms. He didn't want me to approach the dancers, but he would speak to them on my behalf. I felt more confident about marketing in other clubs after experiencing a fairly positive reception at this one. And so I did. Each club was different. One club had a bouncer who wouldn't let me get past the front reception area. The parking lot was packed with cars in the middle of the day—and in the middle of the week. He did take my brochures and promotional materials.

At another club, the manager let me go into the dressing room. I spoke with a couple of dancers and offered them a special Botox deal if they also received dermal filler. Again I left my brochures and contact information.

I drove to another club across town. This one was so dark, I stood in the entryway for some time while my eyes adjusted; even then, I could hardly see the people at the bar. The general manager agreed my services would be something her dancers could use. She took my information. But I still met resistance when I asked if I could talk with the dancers.

I went to a total of ten clubs. I wondered what the point was of marketing in gentlemen's clubs. If it was to get me out of my comfort zone, then I succeeded. If it was to help me change my perception, then I succeeded.

Another aesthetician, who had just graduated from school, went with me to wedding stores and baby stores to offer day spa and salon specials for bridal and baby showers. We found that the bridal stores were run by corporations that forbade marketing by outside vendors. The baby stores were more receptive; however, permission to market our services had to be cleared first. We never heard back from them.

I prayed and practiced Tai Chi and the gentle movement of Qigong every night. Zaysan had told me my life would change with Qigong. With a positive state of mind, I knew my life would take a new direction. It had to. It was just a matter of when.

A visiting aesthetician gave me the name and number of an energy healer, life coach, and Reiki master and suggested I call her. When we spoke on the phone, we both found it difficult to explain exactly how we healed people. We agreed to exchange healing services with one another. She came to my office, and I gave her a one-hour healing session, placing my hands in the air above her body while she lay on the reclined aesthetician chair. My hands moved in symbols above her body, without my control. After the session, we talked and discovered we shared something in common. She studied at the Barbara Brennan School of Healing, and Elizabeth Kuester graduated from the same school.

The next week, I went to her office in Phoenix. I spent some time trying to verbalize what was bothering me about the med spa, the changing economy, and my concern for the day spa and salon success. I also received a beautiful healing session sitting in a chair while she stood behind me with her hands on my shoulders. I felt a very subtle, gentle integration within my energy systems.

When we spoke the next day, she told me that when she came to me for her healing session, she had been tired all week. After the session, she felt revitalized and healthy. She had been seeing a chiropractor for her lower back pains without any lasting success. After the session with me, her pain was completely gone. She said, "Barb, you have the ability to remove what is causing back pain. I can't do this. I will recommend my clients with lower back pain to you."

I was blessed to have experienced this woman's gentle art of healing. I truly feel her healing gift helped me to walk through the closure of the medical spa with grace. I didn't become ill from the stress, and I remained optimistic about the direction of my life.

All the marketing strategies I used produced a modest number of customers, but not enough to sustain a business. If it weren't for prayer, healing, and practicing Qigong every night, I probably would have cracked up from the stress. When my money was almost all gone, I closed the business at the end of July.

During the five months I was in business, several times I sat alone in my office, asking God why I didn't have enough customers. It's easy to blame the economy. It's easy to blame myself. But I'm not a victim, and neither is anyone else on this planet. I didn't have anger, only disappointment. I had accepted the risk. I had also asked for and accepted this experience. If I had the chance to go back in time, I would do it again because it was worth it—though I didn't understand all this at the time.

I don't have anger toward Chloe; instead, I love her. She helped me to experience a profound lesson in trusting that I will be okay, no matter what. Just think what she risked when she entered into this venture with me. She was as optimistic as I was. She had been in this business for many years and was successful. She had entered our medical spa practice not only for herself and the day spa and salon owners, but also for me. She taught me a lot about developing the divine feminine within myself, about the aesthetics business, about standing up for what I believe in and being courageous. She taught me how to survive and walk through the darkest of experiences. As I watched her go through her custody battle, she taught me about the depth of a mother's love for her son. How can I not appreciate the role she played in my life?

My heart chakra opens wide when I remember Chloe. Isn't that the true measure of a person's contribution to another's experience? I learned that how we affect one another's life experience is far more important than money or objects of luxury.

I grew in those months. In other lives, I was successful in business and politics. Perhaps I wanted to experience the opposite of success in this one. I really don't know for sure. I can put all of my effort and energy into a project, and it still may not turn out the way I had planned. Perhaps something greater is coming my way. And this is why I keep asking God, *"What's next?"* Asking this two-word question gave me support and strength to stay in the present moment and move forward.

Chapter 16

MOTHER MARY

In the beginning of August 2008, it was time to put my home on the market. I began packing the contents of my house into boxes. I hired a real estate agent who practices feng shui in her business of selling homes. We decided the best direction for my house was a short sale. While other homeowners in subdivisions were walking out of their houses after partially destroying them—defacing the walls, ripping out light fixtures, and taking appliances—I felt no desire to engage in such behavior. I did receive a foreclosure notice, but I knew in my heart the house would sell. I could feel it.

I cleaned and blessed my house. I blessed the new owner coming to buy it. I arranged for a storage unit to hold my furniture and boxes until I figured out what I was going to do next. A friend of mine who owned a moving company graciously moved my belongings into storage.

My mother called me with panic in her voice and said, "You've got to come over here and stay with us." She was afraid I would be homeless and on the street.

I told her, "It's okay. I'm making arrangements. I will be okay." I appreciated and accepted her offer to let Galileo and me stay in the guest room.

I hired a headhunter to help me secure another job. Several days later, the headhunter sent me to an insurance company in Phoenix. I arrived early and completed an application in the employment office. A supervisor and a manager told me they would conduct the interview together in one of the conference rooms. When the supervisor attempted to turn the light on, it flickered for a moment, but remained off. She tried again. No light. She walked out to find another room for the interview.

The manager and I walked into the darkened room. I turned on the light switch, and the light remained on. The manager exclaimed, "Look, she's a light worker!"

In that moment, I knew what the universe was telling me; I understood this interview would not produce a positive result for my employment. But I still wanted to see how I fared in an interview.

The headhunter called me later that week with the news: "You're overqualified." I understood I wasn't meant to return to the insurance field at this time, and being overqualified was a gentle and diplomatic way of saying, "We didn't choose you." I felt comfortable with this.

Before Galileo and I moved out of our home, I contacted a nurse recruiter for Hawaii. I asked her, "What do I need to do to be in a position to work in a hospital on the Big Island?"

She said, "Recertification in advanced cardiac life support will put you in that position. I can help you acquire work as a nurse—with an apartment and a rental car paid for."

Galileo and I moved to my parents' home in August 2008. I knew this would be a temporary stay while I searched for a job. My house was empty and clean. I returned every two days to water the outdoor plants and trees and to check the air-conditioning and lights. Real estate agents were showing the house to clients. I received several offers, but they were not serious enough to buy the house: the offers were too low. Investors were looking for bargains.

In September, a friend asked if I would pick him up at the airport when he returned from a business trip in the evening. He said, "I'd rather give you the money than a taxicab driver." So I agreed to meet him at the airport at eleven at night.

I left my parents' home at ten o'clock and drove down Thirty-Fifth Avenue to Dunlap. When I approached the intersection, the traffic light turned yellow. I watched two vehicles in the opposite direction with turning signals on begin to turn right. I saw no other cars coming toward me in the other lanes, so I began my turn. In the next instant, a vehicle pulled out from behind the other two cars, passed them, entered the intersection, and went through it.

Already in my turn, I couldn't stop my Ford Expedition fast enough. I pressed on the brake pedal as hard as I could, but it wasn't enough. I struck the driver's door head-on with my vehicle. I heard screeching tires and the impact of metal on metal. I knew the air bag would deploy and abrade my face, so I blocked it with my right arm, bruising my right hand. I sat in my car, dazed and upset, and yet I was more concerned about the welfare of the people in the other car.

My car's hood was bent up. The windshield was smashed. The grill, bumper, and left front headlamp were smashed out. I was grateful the engine and radiator still worked.

Two officers in a police car at the intersection had witnessed the accident. The officer moved my vehicle to the parking lot of a convenience store on the corner. I saw the other people standing, nodding their heads, while talking with the police. I knew they had soft-tissue injuries from the jolt of the impact, and we all would be sore the next day.

This accident was my fault, and I received a citation. I accepted full responsibility, and I told the officer, "Thank you for being here, and God bless you." My auto service towed my car to my parents' house. I called my friend and left a message on his voice mail about the accident.

I prepared for bed with an ice pack on my bruised, swollen hand. With my hand elevated on a pillow, I prayed for the people whose vehicle I hit. I sent healing energy to them and myself. I forgave myself. I didn't understand why this accident occurred. I had no job and now I didn't have a drivable vehicle to search for work. *"Okay, what's next, God?"*

I had received an unusual message from my angels two months before the accident: *"Renew your passport now."*

Surprised, I said, *"Why? I'm not going anywhere. I don't even have the money to travel abroad, but I know you are giving me this message for a reason."* I obtained the forms online and sent my old passport with the renewal application to the passport office.

I sought the expertise of a credit counseling agency to help me determine if I should file for bankruptcy or not. The two female counselors who looked at my situation said the best solution, given my circumstances, was to file Chapter 11. They were very positive people. They agreed with me when I said, "I will rise above this. It may take me some time, but it will happen."

I was fortunate to have the chance to wipe the points from my driving record for the accident by attending a five-hour traffic school class. I found five classes in the area and called the last one on the list. I reserved my name for a morning class and purchased the money order for the class fee.

On September 28, a Sunday morning, I drove to the Comfort Inn Suites hotel in Peoria in my dad's truck and parked in the lot behind the hotel. Paint chipping off exposed the bare gray metal underneath this old vehicle. The door didn't lock. Well, actually, if you locked the door, it wouldn't open again without a crowbar. And the only way to close the door was to slam it shut. The tires had very little tread left on them. Still, I was grateful for just having an automobile to drive to the class. I wasn't in a position to impress anyone, and I had no desire to.

A man in a light-gold colored Lexus SUV parked in the space next to me at the exact time I pulled up. I stepped out of the truck and slammed the door shut. I walked across the parking lot and around the north side, to the east-facing front doors. Other people were walking in the same direction. I was cognizant of the man walking about fifteen feet behind me, but I didn't bother to look around because I was focused on the traffic school class and moving forward in my life.

I entered the conference room, which was more than half full of people. I put my water bottle on a chair near the back door and walked up to the front of the classroom to confirm my attendance and hand in the money order. I sat in my seat between two men. Soon the room filled to standing room only.

The five-hour class was conducted with humor and common sense. This class was not only for my review of driving information, it was also a social occasion. I don't say this meaning I was looking to hook up with someone. Rather, we were all gathered with a common goal—to erase the driving points off our record. I looked around the room and saw people from all walks of life: young and old, skinny and fat, short and tall, bored and bright-eyed.

What I didn't notice was the driver of the Lexus sat next to me. We made small talk during the class. Nothing more. I enjoyed listening to his accent when he spoke. During the break I asked him where he was from.

"Switzerland."

I replied, "Switzerland? How wonderful!" Pleasant memories of chocolate eggs and animal characters made out of marzipan rushed into my mind, along with images of snow-covered mountains, accordions, alpine horns, and cheese with holes. I smiled and made a point to look at the name at the top of his paper. Peter.

When the class concluded, I walked out to the hotel lobby and spoke with the desk clerk while I waited for Peter to come out of the classroom. I wanted to say good-bye out of obligation and courtesy since we had shared half of the day together. More than that, I felt a connection with him on another level, but I couldn't put my finger on it.

Meanwhile, Peter was detained in the classroom with instructor, Alex. Everyone had to make sure their documents were in order for the class to count and the driving points to be erased. He wasn't sure if all of his documents were what the instructor wanted. Alex carefully leafed through the stack of papers, searching the forms. At last, Peter walked into the hotel lobby.

I was happy to see him again. We walked out of the hotel together, and as we stood between our vehicles, he asked me, "Would you like to go have lunch?"

I paused for a moment. I explained about my plans to trim rosebushes at my friend Joan's house. Her arthritis made pruning difficult for her. But I thought I could postpone the trimming. As I sat on this fence of indecision, a voice within me said, *"Say yes."* And I did. We agreed to meet at a local Italian restaurant down the street.

Peter and I discovered we both love to travel and hike. After selling his moving business in Bern, he had purchased a custom off-road motor home and had it transported by ship to Jacksonville, Florida. With two years of English language study in school, he began traveling westward through the southern states. He refined his ability to speak English as he met more Americans to talk with. He visited the national parks in Utah, California, and Arizona. When he arrived in Wickenburg, Arizona, in the winter of 1993, he met a couple of Swiss living there.

Peter fell in love with the desert—a total opposite of the lush green hills and majestic Alps he grew up in. A real estate agent showed him several homes before he settled on buying the historic fifty-acre Sombrero Ranch. He bought the ranch and its five-bedroom home that was built in 1937. Peter then taught himself about running a bed-and-breakfast. He purchased furniture, numbered the room doors, and came up with a Swiss-style breakfast menu. In 1995, he opened the Sombrero Ranch B & B. Peter hosted weddings and offered the ranch as a place for families of residents of the eating disorder and rehab centers in Wickenburg to stay.

In the five years he ran the bed-and-breakfast, only one customer complained—that it was too quiet.

Peter and I were both divorced and available to start a new relationship. We both had been praying for someone special to enter our lives. We were both in the middle of making plans to move away—me to Hawaii and he to Switzerland. We exchanged business cards with our e-mail addresses. He asked me if he could call me, and I agreed to receive his phone call late in the afternoon of the following day. I had no expectations. I was satisfied just to have lunch with a nice man who offered to buy me one.

Still searching for employment, I applied for a job as a medical claim review nurse at a hospital in downtown Phoenix. Since my vehicle was still in the shop, I borrowed my dad's truck again for the interview. It was noon, close to 104 degrees, and I was dressed in a white long-sleeve cotton blouse and navy-blue straight skirt with a hemline just above the knee. I was driving seventy miles per hour on the 101 Freeway, heading east, when I noticed a knocking sound. Then suddenly the right rear tire went flat. I pulled over to the emergency lane.

A man in a pickup truck stopped and looked at the tire. "You can make it to the Fifty-One and pull over for help." I thanked him for his assessment and advice. Isn't it amazing how our angels show up just at the right moment?

Driving carefully, I managed to merge with the traffic and turn onto State Route 51 and pull over on a large area of concrete. A patrol officer pulled his car up behind me and began changing the tire. He called for the backup emergency service vehicle with an air compressor so he could fill up the spare. With my clothes sopping wet and sweat dripping down my face and neck, I called the recruiter and rescheduled the interview for that Thursday. Because I was very grateful for the officers' assistance, I asked for their business cards and later sent a letter to their supervisors, expressing my gratitude.

I was disappointed the flat tire had prevented me from arriving at my interview on time and with a fresh appearance. On Thursday morning, I received a recorded computer message saying the interview wouldn't happen because they had already selected someone for the position. So there again, I received a message that I wasn't to work in the insurance business at this time. More doors were closing.

I had searched for a body shop to repair my Ford Expedition. My Tai Chi grandmaster gave me the name of a body repair specialist. This guy was really good at restoration; in ten days, I had my Expedition back, looking as it had eight years before—new from the dealership showroom.

Peter and I began corresponding by e-mails and talking on our cell phones. He asked me out for lunch again. We agreed to meet at Mimi's Café, a favorite for both of us. We pulled up in the parking lot at the same time. Synchronicity struck again.

When I returned to my parents' home, I drove my vehicle into the driveway and turned off the engine. I sat there for a moment because I could feel an energetic presence in front of my abdomen. I called Peter on my cell phone and said, "Peter, I can feel you energetically! You're right here with me!"

He replied, "Yes, I can feel this too."

Peter and I fell deeply in love, and he asked me and Galileo to move into his hilltop home. In the beginning of our courtship, he said he'd made a point to sit next to me in the traffic school.

I asked him, "What sparked your interest in me?"

He replied, "The minute I saw you, I wanted to know who you were. When we walked to the front of the hotel, I could feel your energy all the way across the parking lot. I felt an overwhelming urge to find out who you are. I thought it odd that a nice woman would be driving an old, beat-up truck. That's why I made sure I sat next to you. After you left the class, I panicked while Alex slowly searched the forms, one by one. I thought to myself, *Hurry up, Alex. I'm going to miss my chance! What do I do? If I don't have the documents in order, then I'm screwed. But I'm screwed if I miss her and don't have her phone number.* Alex finally found the papers. I bolted out of the classroom, ran down the hall, sprinted around the corner, and stopped when I saw you waiting in the lobby."

When he told me this, I remembered a woman I'd met at Costco three years before. She predicted a man would enter my life, and he would love me. She said, "Barbara, your aura is very bright and extends way out there. It's important you remain very positive, like the beacon of a lighthouse in a storm. That is how he will find you."

What I find interesting is that my aura was still bright, even though I was walking through a dark time in my life. My light remains bright because deep down, I remain positive, no matter what happens.

In March of 2009, I filed Chapter 11 bankruptcy. As soon as I filed the papers with the court, the phone calls from the debt collectors stopped. And then I received a letter in the mail from an accounting firm. I held the unopened envelope between my hands, palms together in prayer form. I asked my angels, *"What is this all about?"*

I heard a gentle voice. *"You are not going to like this, but do not worry. All will be taken care of."*

I said, "Okay," opened the envelope, and read the letter requesting documents for a bankruptcy court case audit. My bankruptcy was being audited. The letter requested I send copies of documents I had submitted to the court and letters explaining more details to the auditor. I gave my lawyer a copy of the request. I didn't panic. Instead I trusted that all of this would work out. Later, in court, he would tell me that he had never had a client audited before.

I received a request to explain about some alleged property I owned. I read the documents they sent and saw they had confused me with another Barbara Becker in another state. I signed a notarized affidavit stating I didn't own property in that state and sent additional information to the auditing firm.

When the audit was complete, the accountant accused me of misrepresentation by pocketing the $157,000 from the short sale of my home. I was also accused of not reporting 401(k) money that I had used to pay bills and survive before I closed my aesthetic business. I sent this letter to my attorney.

I didn't understand the logic behind the auditor's conclusion. The way I saw it, if I had kept the money from the sale of the house, I wouldn't even need to file bankruptcy in the first place. In a short sale, the mortgage company or bank receives the money from the new lender. The seller is left out of the loop. I had disclosed on the bankruptcy forms about the 401(k) amount I used to live on. I did understand, on a higher level, that this audit was a test for me—a test in trust that the truth would prevail and it would all work out. Since I had no control over the outcome, I gave it up to God.

My attorney sent a letter to the bankruptcy court trustee and the accounting firm performing the audit. He asked on what grounds the auditor had legal authority to render judgments in my case. He also reminded all the parties involved in my case that I didn't withhold information or receive any money from the short sale of the house.

While the bankruptcy was going on, another loss occurred. On February 18, 2009, at 8:00 p.m., Galileo asked to be let outside for the last time. I opened the door, and he never returned. I understood that wild animals around the ranch could attack Galileo. Trying to convey this fact to Galileo was another matter. He was street smart, but not "country smart." When he didn't show up at the kitchen door the next morning, we called the local vets and the Humane Society. Just in case Galileo's homing instinct kicked in and he became disoriented and walked back to our previous home, I called my previous next-door neighbor, who had four cats. This had happened before, when I was a teenager. My family's cat walked four and a half miles back to our previous home just after we moved.

I waited to hear for my bankruptcy discharge. I contacted the court and found out the bankruptcy trustee hadn't responded to the audit outcome within the statutory guidelines. My case was dismissed by default. In June of 2009, I received the bankruptcy discharge signed by the judge.

Peter took me to Switzerland to meet his family and friends in the fall of 2009. That's when I understood why my angels gave me the message to renew my passport twelve months earlier. Peter and I traveled through Switzerland, western Austria and northern Italy.

Two weeks before we left Switzerland, on a cool fall morning, Peter and I left our hotel in Ittigen. It was September 28, our one-year anniversary of meeting each other at traffic school. As we walked toward the car in the parking lot, a cat with the same markings and color as Galileo walked up to Peter and purred. The cat then walked over to me and rolled onto his back as I stroked his belly.

"Hi, Mama. Happy anniversary."

I felt chills through my body, confirming it was Galileo. I was happy he had come back in physical form, even for that brief moment, to say hello again.

This cat hung around and walked up to me each time I performed Qigong in the hotel garden. He told me he was okay, and he was there for a visit. The night before we left for America, he returned one more time to the parking lot to say good-bye. I thanked him for coming. He reminded me I could talk to him anytime because he is in my heart universe.

When I walked back into the hotel, the desk clerk said to me, "We don't know who that cat belongs to. He just showed up here a couple of weeks ago."

I recollected the date of two weeks before: the twenty-eighth. I replied to the clerk's comment, "It's okay, I know where he's from."

Galileo left my life just as he had entered it, unexpectedly. His time with me is a reminder for each of us to appreciate what we have in the present moment because we don't know what's going to happen next. I also learned about our perceptions with one another. Even though he was thought of as a bully by other people, to me, he was a loving and wise cat. Maybe he lived up to my perception, and that's why he behaved in a loving manner with me. I was fortunate to have been chosen by a stargazing bully to teach me more about love.

In March of 2010, I received a "kick-in-the-butt" reading from a spiritual advisor in Prescott, Arizona. The reading felt uncomfortable, and I wondered when in the reading I would feel the warm and fuzzy part. It was a message for me to get out there and lead people through guidance again. At the end of the reading, I stated, "This will all come about, when my book is written and published." As I spoke these words, the whole room lit up with energy and both of our bodies were buzzing with vibration. The advisor smiled and said, "Yes, yes!"

While walking down the hallway in the house on the ranch, I heard my angels tell me, "Finish your projects." I had sewing projects and arts and crafts that I've been carrying around for many years, but never got around to completing them. I gave away the projects I knew I would not create and finished two cotton quilted jackets. My angels know I love to create with art through my painting and sewing. These projects for me are distractions to the work of writing a book. I also asked my angels to help me stay focused on writing. Every time I went into meditation, my angels showed me a book. Sometimes I would see a feather pen writing on a page in a book. This support helped me to keep my deadlines and maintain my priorities.

I researched on the Internet how to write a book. I purchased two books on writing an autobiography and finding my voice. I wrote every day and tried different formulas for writing. I found authors who recommended devoting a number of hours in a day to writing. Others recommended writing a certain number of pages per day. I focused on one chapter at a time and let the words flow into my fingers on the keyboard.

In November of 2010, I received a message from my Higher Self. "Pack your bags; leave with joy." I didn't know where I was going. Still, I heeded their message, and packed all of my belongings into boxes. Peter understood I had to create my own wealth and continue on my path as a healer and teacher. While we both wanted to stay together, surviving financially meant we had to live apart. I began my search for a job, any job, to create the money flow again.

On the other side of bankruptcy is the process of rebuilding monetary wealth and credit. Through my research and the help of a financial advisor, I rebuilt my place of financial comfort. This meant I had to step back into the corporate environment for employment and move back to the Phoenix area in April of 2011. I accepted a position as a medical claim review nurse at TriWest Healthcare Alliance. I came to that job with a renewed sense of gratitude and joy. Every morning, sitting at my desk in a cubicle, I prayed that every claim I touched, everyone involved receives a healing and blessing. At lunch, I prayed and blessed my food. This employment provided the money I needed to publish my book and to live in a comfortable apartment. I began tithing my income to charities. I received unexpected bonuses. Peter and I appreciated our time together on the weekends even more.

Walking through a personal bankruptcy gives a person strength and courage. It changes perceptions about money and people, and our relationship with money and the world. We find the true value of objects and appreciate the kindness and generosity of others more than we did before.

Peter and I returned to Europe in the late summer of 2010, and I received a message to travel to a cathedral. On September 2, at my request, Peter drove us to the Shrine of Our Lady of Einsiedeln. Located about twenty miles southeast of Zurich, this enormous church is dedicated to Mother Mary. This shrine has a Benedictine monastery and the relics of a saint.

As the legend goes, a monk named Meinrad left a local monastery in the ninth century to build a hermitage in the forest that would later become Einsiedeln. He was given a miracle-working statue of Mary, also known as the Black Madonna, by the Abbess Hildegarde of Zurich. The monk became well known for his holiness and his kindness to many visitors, who gave him gifts.

On January 21, 861, Meinrad was murdered by two thieves for his accumulated treasure at the hermitage. The murderers were apprehended after two black ravens followed them into town and squawked loudly, drawing attention to them. Later a group of Benedictine monks transformed the little hermitage into a chapel. The bishop who was to perform the consecration of the chapel received a vision of the church filled with

a brilliant light as Christ approached the altar. It's said that Jesus consecrated the chapel on September 14, 948. The next day, when the bishop
walked to the chapel to perform the ceremony, he heard a voice saying
the chapel had already been divinely consecrated. This was confirmed
by Pope Leo VIII sixteen years later. Many miracles were attributed to
the Black Madonna statue, and pilgrimages began after AD 1000. St.
Meinrad is now considered the saint of hospitality.

When Peter and I entered the cathedral, we went off in different
directions. There was a sign posted to remind people this was a place
of respect and prayer and that no photography was allowed. I walked
directly to the black marble shrine in the back. I was guided to walk
over and kneel down in the middle of the pews. I looked up and saw the
Black Madonna statue. Because of the amount and brilliance of the gold
backdrop and of sculptured bolts of energy blasting out from behind the
statue, I felt the energy from the gold. (I had felt the same when I visited
the gold in the Museo del Oro in Peru. Creating this frequency is one of
the reasons why the Catholic Church uses gold in the decoration of the
altars and paintings.)

I said prayers quietly to myself. "Mother Mary, if you want to use me
as a channel for healing the people gathered here today, let it be so." I
thanked her for all she does for humanity—past, present, and future. I sat
back in the pew and felt someone touching my left hand. I opened my eyes,
but there was no one close to me. There were people sitting all around in
the pews, and there were people in wheelchairs. No one was talking.

I breathed deeply and went deeper into meditation. I could feel the
energy about to enter my body. And then it happened. My arms sprang up
in the air in rapid movement. With the mathematical language running
through my body, I went momentarily unconscious. And then it was over.
My arms slowly returned to my lap, and I sat in an energy field of harmony and bliss. I felt energy returning to my body, and slowly I regained
full consciousness. No one rushed to me or looked at me. I was told by my
guide that everyone was unconscious during this healing.

I stood up and walked up the center aisle to the main altar in the
cathedral. People huddled in what appeared to be a tour group in front of
me. They were laughing, looking up, and pointing to the architecture and
the painting on the ceiling. I prayed and gave thanks to God. Looking
up, I saw two stuffed black crows on a ceiling niche. This must have been
what the people were laughing about.

I walked over and stood in front of the altar dedicated to St. Anna. At the top of the altar is a sculpted pyramid with an eye in the middle. It reminded me of the tip of the pyramid on the back of a one-dollar bill. I looked around and didn't notice any other pyramid-shaped decorations. As we were standing there, a priest and someone who had a bundle of keys unlocked the ornate black wrought-iron gates in front of the altar and walked in. They stood there talking. In fact, all of the altars, including the main altar at the head of the cathedral, were cut off from the petitioners by locked gates.

As I walked around, studying the architecture, I was filled with awe of the coral-pink color and texture of the sculptures. There was so much to ponder and reflect on. To me, this cathedral far surpassed the ornateness of St. Peter's in the Vatican. The cathedral was transmitting a feminine energy. Before we left, I lit two candles and said my prayers.

On the flight home to America, I experienced a heart-opening event. At thirty-five thousand feet, my heart chakra opened suddenly. Through my third eye, I saw billions of tiny hearts exploding away from my body in all directions. The immense amount of love I felt for everyone and everything on the planet was overwhelming. I squeezed Peter's hand, tears flowing down my face. I kept repeating to him, "I love everyone." My entire body shook from the energy flowing through Peter. After about fifteen minutes of this surging energy, I returned to my normal state and went to sleep.

It is possible that this heart opening was the event Dr. Peebles had told me about in 2005. The intense realization of the amount of love I feel for everyone on Earth hit me really hard. It was as if I were birthing myself through my heart. Another transition had occurred deep within me.

Chapter 17

WHO I AM

B ack in 2005, Sharon Stone was interviewed by James Lipton on the series *Inside the Actors Studio*. She told a story that confirmed my belief that we are here to learn about love. She sat at her friend's bedside when he was dying of AIDS. At the moment of death, he closed his eyes and stopped breathing. A short time afterward, he opened his eyes and said to her, "Sharon, it's all about love." And then he died. She was touched by his effort to come back for that brief moment and deliver this message. She, in turn, shared it with us. Love helps us to understand one another. It removes barriers in communications. Love teaches us to forgive. And most of all, love heals.

I'm here to learn more and teach about self-love. I'm also here to experience the human condition, learn from my experiences, change my perspectives, and live my life purpose in service to others. I've had lessons to help me see the true meaning behind a person's behavior, and that behavior is always based in love, even when it doesn't feel like it. One of my life experiences illustrates this lesson.

While working as a medical claim review nurse, a female coworker was saying derogatory things to me and harassing me regarding work issues. I was feeling awful and trying my best to stay positive, but it just wasn't working. I didn't realize it at the time, but this coworker was reflecting myself back to me. My reality was that I was the person not staying positive, and I was beating myself up. She was "sacrificing" herself to give me this message.

I was very determined to change this negative reality of mine. So I sat at my desk, and for five minutes, I concentrated on feeling good, happy, and helpful. I concentrated on feeling love, compassion, and forgiveness for myself. I remembered a happy moment with my husband from one of our travels abroad. I soaked up these feelings. When I felt my emotions and vibration had changed, I sent positive feelings to that coworker for five minutes. Then I let it go and returned to my work.

Within the next five minutes, the coworker came to my cubicle and asked, "Do you need help? Is there anything I can do for you, to help you in your work?" Of course, I accepted her help and expressed my gratitude. She lightened my workload.

When she left my cubicle, I sat there with my mouth open and thought, *Oh my God, this really works!* We can change our reality. We can change others when we change ourselves. I'm eternally grateful for this coworker's involvement in my lesson. And if I can do it, anyone can.

Acknowledging and changing one's vibration and mental state may be one of the hardest processes to go through. That's because the negative feelings inside are very strong. In the beginning, it took great effort to change my emotional being from negative to positive. But the more I practiced it, the easier it became.

We come to this planet over and over until we have completed all of our missions and learn to love ourselves and others unconditionally. I remember Willaru telling our group, "Stay on your path, and don't look back." I channeled this same message to Genevieve, the flight attendant, on the flight back to America. This message serves to help us stay on our spiritual growth track rather than focus on regrets and unforgiving situations. What we hold on to causes the cancer cells within all of us to manifest into disease.

We must be positive no matter what happens. Even when we walk through depression, anger, frustration, hopelessness, and other low vibrations, we must strive to seek the higher frequency of hope and positivity. We must forgive ourselves and other people. Forgiveness is one of the ways to release ourselves from our cycle on the karmic wheel. Even the entities or spirits that have lashed out at me through anger and vile statements from people have served to build my character and strength.

They appear to me now as an illusion or false pretense of being demonic. Of course they are nothing to fear because the light within us is far more loving and powerful. They are no more powerful than I, and very possibly, vice versa. We are all united in this grand experience in the third dimension of soul growth.

When I wrote this book, I had to look back to tell my story and to learn from my past. I find it interesting that I have two different ways of looking back: one, as a human, experiencing the emotions and consequences of my lessons, and two, as a spiritually awakened being, understanding the benefits, the karma, the deeper meaning and purpose of the experiences, and the individual's (people and animals) role in helping me to find and feel more love for myself and others. This is why I'm grateful for everyone who has touched my life—in positive and negative ways. It was all meant to be. Life happens.

If we're here as spirits having a human experience, we are meant to feel all the emotions. We're meant to walk through the tough lessons and realize it's about love. I can't remember exactly when it dawned on me that our most excruciatingly painful and uncomfortable experiences promote significant growth in us and serve to release us from that which binds and encloses us. This is why every night when I pray to God, I tell Him I'm grateful for all of my experiences—the joyful ones and the difficult ones. When we acknowledge we are meant to struggle, the struggle disappears, or at least lessens to a dull roar, where it doesn't bother us. I perceive lessons as merely a project I'm working on. And it doesn't matter whether I get it right or wrong. It's the process. It's the journey.

I've been a conformer for most of my life. I've conformed and assimilated into the collective in order to be accepted and liked. But I've learned that life isn't about being just like everybody else. It's about being who I really am and not caring what others think about me. After all, what people think about me is really none of my business. How do I know this? Because when I look at book reviews, blog comments, and opinions rendered by professionals, common folk, and everyone else in between, there is a full variety of perspectives, from the negative to the positive. We all have a right to our opinion. Since we all transition out of this life and back to our spirit form, nothing really matters. Eventually we will all learn and discover we are love. We are the truth we seek. We are One.

I'm more than just a human named Barbara Becker. I'm a star being. We are all star beings. We are connected to the earth, the stars, the gal-

180

axies, and more. We are connected to everything. Astrophysicist Neil deGrasse Tyson wrote that hydrogen, oxygen, carbon, and nitrogen are from stars that ended in a supernova explosion and that these are the four most common elements of life on Earth.[11] I've experienced my "star self," from intuitives telling me I am a star being, to me feeling and seeing a sparkly, pulsating brilliant light, in the formation of a star, inside my body while walking down a sidewalk.

We come to Earth through our mother's womb after we sign up for a set of lessons. We agree who will be our parents, our families, our friends, and our foes for the purpose of learning through life experiences. A veil of forgetfulness is placed over our consciousness. We decide our actions. We are given the freedom of choices: To live or to die. To step forward or to retreat. To love or fear. To smile or cry. And then, add the ingredient of non-control into the mixture. We are not in control. We think we are, but we are not. We make our choices, we take action, and then we leave it up to God. Some doors will close, and others will open. This is how we learn about trust and faith. This is where I find peace and the excitement of life, all at the same time.

I have a gift of healing, and it's still unfolding. This mathematical language inside of me is speaking constantly. I have the ability to push it back to where it doesn't interfere with my day-to-day activities and conversations. And I have the ability to bring it forward into my vocal cords and speak it for healing purposes. I can turn it off and back on. And because I've been given this gift, I'm obligated to share it with as many as possible. To be of service to others brings me joy. And my gratitude brings me happiness.

We exist in other dimensions and parallel universes. Everyone holds the divine spark of God's light and love within them. The journey to our hearts starts when we realize we're all connected to one another. This connection is the reason we give loving allowance for everyone to be who they are and for us to be who we are. We have a uniqueness about us. We each bring to the collective table our culture, our personalities, our skills and talents, our beliefs, and an immense capacity to love ourselves and each other.

---

11   Neil deGrasse Tyson, "The Cosmic Perspective," Hayden Planetarium, http://www. haydenplanetarium.org/tyson/read/2007/04/02/the-cosmic-perspective, previously published in *Natural History Magazine*, April 2007.

Upon meditation, I realize there is a portion of humans who desire to be "asleep" until it's time to awaken their consciousness. For me, it was at age forty-two. I have read about and met people who have been consciously aware of their sixth senses and psychic/healing abilities from the time they were children. This is due to the balance required to assist the planetary ascension in a gentle manner. There is no good or bad, no wrong or right about living one's life awake or asleep. Everyone is part of this. Everyone is performing their contribution to this balance.

All of the behaviors, thoughts, and actions that I committed while not understanding I could have been more compassionate, loving, and forgiving were simply meant to be. If this world were all peace and harmony, how would we know the difference from anger, hate, and imbalance? And yet, when I look at the bigger picture, I ask myself, *Is there a difference between good and bad, right and wrong?* If I am to believe that there is no separation between me, other people, animals, plants, rocks, the weather, vibrations, concepts, and oral and written statements, then there is no difference. The difference is here to help us learn and process our lessons of compassion, love, and forgiveness. We must have differences, arguments, war, and other disruptive events until we humans, as a collective community, transition to a higher vibration of love and peace. And the most wonderful news I share with you, is this transition is already occurring within each of us.

I am healer and channel. I am teacher and student. I am Love. I am Light. I am the Beloved. I am One. It does not matter to me what you have done, or not done, said or not said, thought or not thought, I love you.

ABOUT THE AUTHOR

Barbara Becker was a former critical care nurse, who works with the angelic realm, teaching, guiding, and channeling healing for clients. She lives in Arizona. Please visit her website at www. BarbaraBeckerHealing.com

Made in the USA
Charleston, SC
20 January 2015